The Helpline is Engaged

By
Adwoba Addo-Boateng

The Helpline is Engaged
Adwoba Addo-Boateng

Published By Parables
October, 2018

All Rights Reserved. No part of this book may be reproduced or utilized in any form or by any means, electronic or mechanical, including photocopying, recording, or by any information storage and retrieval system, without permission in writing from the author.

    ISBN 978-1-945698-79-8
    Printed in the United States of America

Readers should be aware that Internet Web sites offered as citations and/or sources for further information may have been changed or disappeared between the time this was written and the time it is read.

The Helpline is Engaged

By
Adwoba Addo-Boateng

ABOUT THE AUTHOR

Adwoba Addo-Boateng is passionate about teaching the gospel of Christ through practical examples that people can relate to. She strongly believes that we can be the change through Christ. She holds a Bachelor of Arts degree in Psychology and Spanish and a Master of Arts degree in Economic Policy Management from the University of Ghana. She is currently pursuing a PhD in Human and Social Services. She is married with children.

DEDICATION

I dedicate this book to my dearest grand mum, Margaret Nvidah who taught me the value of prayer by setting an example herself. She would wake up every four am to pray each day, in spite of life challenges. A great woman who will relinquish everything to prayer and has all the patience in the world to wait for what God has to say finally. A woman who has been through so much but yet has the peace of God. Yeye, your love, care and support through it all has been enormous. The bond we share is inexplicable, I love you!

ACKNOWLEDGEMENT

I thank the Almighty God, by whose grace I was able to discover and write this book and I thank the Holy Spirit for His guidance and inspiration. It has been an incredible journey.

To my dear brother, Pascal Ledzi Segbefia, I say thank you for introducing me to Christ and never giving up on me. It has been an unveiling year for us all and it was great having you on board.

To my dear husband, Kwaku Addo-Boateng, this idea came at a time when it was tough but you stood by me and became my best supporter. Thank you for believing in me, your criticisms pushed me into doing a good work.

To my lovely gifts from above, Nanahene, Maame Nhyira, Ohemaa Nyamensa and Ewurasika Addo-Boateng thank you for cheering me on. Your prayers and suggestions were a great source of encouragement.

To my dear mum, Lana Moso Osei, you bought me my first book with your meager salary which sparked my love for books. I was so happy that day, you never knew the Author you helped me to become. Thank you for igniting the confidence in me and encouraging me to be stronger in the Lord which pushed me to greater heights.

"Now to Him, who is able to do exceedingly abundantly above all that we ask or think, according to the power that works in us, to Him be glory in the church by Christ Jesus to all generations, forever and ever Amen". (Ephesians 3:20-21)

SYNOPSIS/SUMMARY

When you have a mobile phone irrespective of the brand, you normally call your trusted best friend whom you really love. You call not only when you are in need or have an issue to discuss. There are times you just call to say hello. You chat almost about anything; your day at work, your crushes, your disappointments, your pain, your joy, your wants and your needs. You rely on this great friend for both physical and emotional support. This phone call always makes you feel better and you are always encouraged to call this special person in your life. You use this mobile phone anywhere and anytime, and the communication is still effective. You might have a favourite spot in your house where you enjoy such conversations but it doesn't make or mar the communication but it just makes you feel comfortable. When you cannot chat due to issues with dead battery, insufficient minutes, network failure, phone broken down and among others, you find ways and means of solving the communication hitch. You engage in activities such as recharging the battery, buying more minutes, buying a new phone so that you can chat more. You always make sure the conversation with this person is active despite challenges because you love to talk to this person. When you do this chat with God, it is prayer. Prayer in simple terms is like talking to your best friend. You are able to tell God anything as it flows from your heart. You don't select the information, you tell it as it is, because you can trust Him fully. The phone that you use to call is ever ready you make it active by just picking the phone and making the call and talking to HIM. When placing a call to God we must make sure we have the right number. The right number is Christ and the heart is the speed dialing number anytime you want to talk to God. Moreover, when you call and hear the dialing tone, you have to wait for it to be picked. The dialing tone rings a number of times before it is picked. Sometimes it rings and it is not picked. Other times, just the first ring and it is picked. Whichever way, you just have to wait for the phone to be answered. Prayer goes with patience when you want an answer. Prayer in sum is the outpouring of your heart through Christ and waiting for God's answer in His time according to His will.

Without Christ and the heart the call doesn't go through and the helpline is engaged. ***"I the LORD search the heart and examine the mind, to reward each person according to their conduct, according to what their deeds deserve."*** (Jeremiah 17:10) God loves us so much that He wants us to talk to Him always. God is everyone's trusted best friend, we all have equal access to Him. We can all have a close relationship with Him by talking to Him all the time. ***In all your ways submit to him, and He will make your paths straight*** (Proverbs 3:6).

TABLE OF CONTENTS
INTRODUCTION
CHAPTER ONE
GETTING TO KNOW CHRIST: THE JOURNEY
FINDING THE NARROW PATH; A ROLLER COASTER RIDE
CLEARING THE BUMPS ON THE WAY
SUBMISSION
LETTING GO
DO NOT BE SIN CONSCIOUS
ENTERING THE THRONE ROOM OF GRACE
CHAPTER TWO
THE GENESIS OF PRAYER
AFTER THE FALL
GOD LOOKED AT THE HEART
JESUS IS THE MASTER CLEANER
TURN YOUR SHAME INTO A NAME
WHAT IS PRAYER
WHO SHOULD PRAY
TYPES OF PRAYER
CHAPTER THREE
HOW TO PRAY
PERSONAL PRAYER
GROUP PRAYER
SUBMITTING TO THE HOLY SPIRIT
PLACES TO PRAY
CHAPTER FOUR
WHEN TO PRAY
THE PURPOSE OF PRAYER
THE BUMPY RIDE
CHAPTER FIVE
A HEARTFELT PRAYER
CONTRITE HEART
ABIDING HEART
FAITHFUL HEART

THANKFUL HEART
PURE HEART
A TRUE PRAYER
CHAPTER SIX
GOD'S ANSWER
FIXING THE BROKEN LEG OF THE TABLE
RESTING IN THE FINISHED WORK OF CHRIST
THE GOOD SHEPHERD
DON'T TRY TO UNDERSTAND GOD
AN INSTANT GOD
HE COMES THROUGH AT THE RIGHT TIME
MISFORTUNES CAN BE ANSWERS
PERMISSIVE WILL OF GOD
GOD'S PERFECT WILL
WAITING FOR GOD'S TIMING
CHAPTER SEVEN
THE VALUE OF PRAYER
LETTING GOD IN
WHATEVER GOD DOES IS GOOD
HIS WAY IS NOT YOUR WAY.
BE IN GOD'S WILL
DESIRING A RELATIONSHIP WITH THE FATHER

INTRODUCTION

Life can sometimes be very frustrating and complex; there is a need we want to be met. Unfortunately, the harder we try, there seems to be no way out. There is always something which is not there which we badly desire and we feel it will make us complete. It could be children to save a marriage, a job to make you financially independent, a cure you want for a disease, sometimes you just want peace of mind in a troubled situation and it looks like looking for a needle in a haystack. There was a time, I was faced with a certain challenge in my life, and I did not know where I was heading to. So I resorted to prayer because I had tried all avenues but it did not yield any results.

I prayed all manner of prayers and became very prayerful or so I thought, I realized that the more I prayed, the more I got frustrated, worse of all with no answers and even the situation was getting worse.

I went for all prayer meetings, prayed harder and for long hours. I still wasn't getting answers. I was in the front pew whenever there was a church programme. I even paid all my financial commitments in church and gave good offerings to make my prayers more effective but it was to no avail. Then I began to ask questions; what was I not doing right? Prayer to me, has suddenly become like a struggle with no interest at all, obviously, I wasn't enjoying it.

Why didn't God answer my prayers? I can really pray!!!

Out of my frustration, I called my very good friend one sunny afternoon. What is Prayer? Why does my prayer feel like work? I asked.

He laughed and said unfortunately that is what is happening these days. He asked, Are you a Christian? Are you kidding me? I replied with a question. Who do you think I am? I have been a Christian ever since I was born. Honestly, that question kept on playing in my mind. Then my mind drifted off a bit. Have I truly found Christ in my heart or I just profess Christ on my lips. Did I really know Christ? Sincerely, the answer was no. So what was I praying through? Was I praying for praying sake? Oh, I was caught up in the trend and how did I get there? In 1Timothy 2:5, **Paul said, for there is one God and one mediator between God and mankind, the man Christ Jesus**. My friend concluded that Christianity is a relationship with the father that is God through the son. It is supposed to be you and the father only. If you are hiding behind prayer meetings, church programmes and you do not have an interpersonal relationship with God through the Son, then I am afraid, you are missing it.

Then I asked, what is Prayer?

I remember vividly what he said; Prayer is an outpouring of your heart to your maker which is God and for you being a Christian the outpouring of your heart has to pass through Jesus Christ the son. How will your prayer be answered if you don't even know Christ? He is not in your heart, he concluded. In John 14:5-6, Thomas said to him, Lord, we don't where you are going. so how can we know the way. *Jesus answered, I am the way and the truth and the life. No one comes to the Father except through me.*

Have I poured my heart out to God? Or I was just making ruffling sounds or I was praying according to laid down procedures and rules. What were my motives behind all those prayer meetings? Was I praying for His will to be done or I wanted it done my way? 1st John 5:14-15 says *"This is the confidence we have in approaching God: that if we ask anything according to his will, he hears us. And if we know that he hears us—whatever we ask—we know that we have what we asked of him"*.

It dawned on me that I had made three major blunders. First, I didn't have Christ and secondly I wasn't praying through my heart, finally I wasn't praying for His will to be done in the situation I found myself in. Waiting for an answer in His time was another thing altogether.

Then I realized that I have been a victim of what I would term as "manual work" automatically without result and no peace at all.

Wait a minute; is that the promise of God, when we pray? In **Philippians 4; 6-7 we are told not to be anxious about anything** *but in every situation by prayer and petition, with thanksgiving we should present our requests to God, and the peace of God which transcends all understanding, will guard our hearts and our minds in Christ Jesus.* There was a time when I had a distress call from my daughter's school. The head teacher said my daughter's temperature was running at 40 degrees Celsius. She said: I don't know what to do. I have given her first aid but it doesn't seem to be improving. Can you please come quickly, and then she hanged up. As I was about to hurriedly go to the school. I suddenly felt I shouldn't rush and that God was in control. I decided to worship with a song, as words will fail me. As I sang the song, I felt immediately God was in control. I had received inner rest and I had the peace that can't be understood by human minds. Believing the fact that it is God that saves, frustration wasn't going to save my situation. After a while, the head teacher called and said: Mummy, your daughter is okay, the high temperature has gone down. I sang a song of praise.

There are times, God may not have answered your prayer yet, because the timing is not right but He will give you the peace which can't be understood by human minds. It is not negotiable, it is a promise and this promise can only be achieved if you have Christ and you are praying a genuine prayer and you are waiting for His will to be done. So then, if you pray and you do not have any peace within you and rather you are frustrated then you ask yourself these questions. Do I have Christ? Am I praying from my heart? Am I praying according to the will Of God, Am I waiting for God's answer at His time?

I realized I wasn't alone in this predicament, I felt strongly this book had to come out to educate people on what really prayer is and encourage those who are frustrated by prayer that God still answers prayer. Is your Prayer work? Is your Prayer complicated? Is Prayer wearing you down? Find Christ and pray through the heart according to the will of God and the peace of God that transcends all understanding will be given to you. In *Matthew 7:11 Jesus said; If you, then, though you are evil, know how to give good gifts to your children, how much more will your Father in heaven give good gifts to those who ask him.*

God loves us so much that He gave his only begotten son to come and die for us, why won't He give us all things we ask for, if it is His will and it is His time. We are truly cherished by God and He wants the best for us.

CHAPTER ONE
GETTING TO KNOW CHRIST: THE JOURNEY

How do we find Christ? That is a million dollar question. We can find Christ by abiding in him. In **John 15:4 Jesus said *"Abide in me, and I in you. As the branch cannot bear fruit by itself, unless it abides in the vine, neither can you, unless you abide in me"*.**

Abiding in Christ was an instruction Jesus gave and that is the only way one can be fruitful and most importantly getting to find and know Christ in the process. When you abide you allow Jesus to roll out your life for you and you just move along. So simple, isn't it?

When you begin to abide, he prunes and removes all unnecessary factors affecting the growth of the tree, so that the tree will be even more fruitful and finding Christ is so close. No worries! Jesus is the Gardener. It is not that hard, because he wouldn't prune in such a way that you can't handle. Good news! He brings relief on the way. What a Loving father! He is just emptying the jar deposited in you and refilling it with Christ, So that Christ will be your ALL Dependency. When we were born, society and environment influences us in so many ways that we gradually lose track of the narrow path. In Matthew 7; 13-14, Jesus made mention of two ways of life and He said, ***"Enter by the narrow gate; for wide is the gate and broad is the way that leads to destruction, and there are many who go in by it. Because narrow is the gate and difficult is the way which leads to life, and there are few who find it"***. Man's ultimate destiny on earth is to find the narrow path that leads to who we actually were before we were born. And that narrow path leads to finding Christ. That narrow path is very lonely and sometimes you will be made to believe that it is the wrong path. When you can overcome loneliness, you can overcome anything. Just give up your own way and follow the Lord. Jesus will lead and take you through that journey.

FINDING THE NARROW PATH: A ROLLER COASTER RIDE

Life throws us certain misfortunes and we feel there is no God. Most times these misfortunes can be blessings in disguise. Sometimes we are faced with a grievous situation and finding Christ may be the last on our minds. How do we find Christ in the midst of adversaries?

Communicating with God is a very important key through a personal relationship. Start the process of knowing God in every little way you can by talking to him even if it is just for a minute. Sometimes, in the midst of hardships it is so difficult to talk to God. Turn all your worries into prayer. Pray as the situation is, even "I am not able to pray" is a prayer to God. Sometimes we don't know what to say to God when our faith is challenged. Tell Him; God I am down, I am broken, I don't have the strength to pray, I don't see any sign of light at the end of the tunnel, I am at my saturation point, when I thank you it is not from my heart. Tell God exactly how you feel, let your concerns be known to him. Anything that is in you, just pour it out to God. Put the prayer methodologies aside, it will not help at this moment. Give yourself to the study of the word of God and let the word of God dwell in you. Even if you can't concentrate on the word of God, tell God so. He will help you out no matter what. God wants Christ to be our only consolation. He also makes a way where there seems to be no way. Even if God will pass help through someone, it is someone you can't fathom any help from. By so doing you are trusting God that He is the only help you have even though the reality of the situation is starring in your face. You are only relying on Jesus Christ. Christ will be the only rock on which you stand and all other grounds will be sinking sand.

REMOVING THE BUMPS ON THE WAY
SUBMISSION IN MARRIAGE

In marriage, sometimes we may feel we are married to the wrong partner. We feel our partner is the worst thing that happened to us. Did I not see? We will ask ourselves severally especially when our spouse is behaving in inappropriate ways. Ohemaa met Nana in the university and immediately liked each other; they got married soon after leaving the university. Two years into the marriage, Ohemaa realized that she made a mistake in marrying Nana. They could not have one meaningful conversation, their chats were always characterized by quarrels, arguments and squabbles obviously they were not on the same path. It just wasn't working. Ohemaa needed God in her marriage owing to the fact that she couldn't do it on her own. It was so overwhelming. All the opportunities Ohemaa wanted from God were not forthcoming. She needed to fix the collar of her husband's shirt even though it was difficult and it is only through Christ that it could be done. She let everything go so that God could handle it. All her anger and thoughts were poured out in prayer to the Lord, and then she realized she had to change herself instead of trying to change someone. Ohemaa through Christ turned over a new leaf, she became very meek and in spite of her husband's issues she became very submissive to him. After a while, Ohemaa's husband was changing too and so positively, she was beginning to live an exemplary life for her husband to emulate. It was beautiful! All of a sudden, the opportunities she wanted way back were all opened. It was a beautiful feeling; she has evolved into Christ's beautiful bride. Let's try to love our spouse even if they don't deserve it, for undeserving as we are God loved us enough to give us His only begotten son to die for our sins. Let's try to be the change instead of changing others.

"You hypocrite, first take the plank out of your own eye, and then you will see clearly to remove the speck from your brother's eye". Matthew 7:5. In 1 peter Chapter 3, wives are told to be submissive to their husbands so that their husbands will be won over by their chaste and fear conduct and not by their outward appearance. The hidden person of the wife's heart accompanied by the incorruptible beauty of a gentle and quiet spirit is very precious in the sight of God. When a wife is able to submit to her husband, she has the favour of God. Then in response the husband will also live with his wife with understanding and respecting her. So that their prayers may not be hindered and they will be heirs together of the grace of life.

SUBMISSION TO GOVERNMENT

The fact that you are a Christian doesn't mean you are above the laws or rules of a country. You shouldn't use your freedom as liberty for improper behavior but rather as bond servants of Christ. 1 Peter 2:13 says, ***Submit yourselves to every ordinance of man for the Lord's sake, whether to the king as supreme, or to governors as to those who are sent by evildoers and for the praise of those who do good. For this is the will of God.*** Kofi was a good Christian who worked in investment company. Every employee of where he worked engaged in bribery and corruption. It was like the norm, everyone was doing it. He was tempted severally but his conscience will not allow him. People called him weak and all sort of names but he was still adamant. A few weeks later, government conducted an audit at the firm and all culprits were dealt with accordingly. Kofi feared the Lord and engaging in such acts was abominable as a Christian. He never had the erroneous impression that God will protect him no matter what. He rather used his freedom in Christ to set a good example for others to follow. A few months later Kofi was promoted to an investment manager in the firm. In Matthew 5:16 it says ***In the same way, let your light shine before others, that they may see your good deeds and glorify your Father in heaven***.

SUBMISSION TO MASTERS

Servants should be submissive to their masters with all fear, not only to the good and gentle but also to the harsh, if because of conscience toward God one endures grief and suffering wrongfully, it is commendable. (1 Peter 2:18). No matter the kind of jobs we find ourselves in, we should work as if we are working for the Lord. Nhyira was a lady who worked so hard in her job. She worked as a housekeeper in Mr. and Mrs. Asem's house. She was very dutiful, but the couple always took advantage of her. They paid her less than what she actually deserves. That didn't deter her; she worked as if she was working for the Lord. She was at home one day when a wealthy friend of

Mr. Asem came to visit. He was stricken by her beauty and most importantly her hard work. He decided to marry Nhyira. All efforts to talk him out of it proved futile. They got married in a lavish ceremony. Her hard work paid off. She got something that she wasn't even asking for.

OBEDIENCE TO PARENTS

Children should obey their parents in the Lord, for this is right. Children should honour their father and mother which is the first commandment with a promise. So that it may be well with them and their days may be long on earth. (Ephesians 6:1-3). When you obey your parents; you are doing the will of God. Doing the will of God is one step closer towards getting your prayers answered and finding Christ. A couple I knew was married for ten years without any child. They tried all they could and prayed all manner of prayers but it looked as if God had turned on a deaf ear. They were so miserable; they did not understand why they were not being blessed with a child. Unknowingly to each other, they all had issues against their parents because they felt their parents were not responsible enough. They were very disrespectful to them and didn't regard them as parents. Through guidance and counseling, they felt sorry for being disrespectful and started respecting them and in the following year they had a child. No matter what we think our parents should have done that they didn't. We must learn to obey them for only one reason: you are doing the will of God. When we do the will of God, your business, is His business and He will never let you down.

LETTING GO

Sometimes our prayers are not answered because the passage is blocked. We must learn to forgive no matter what. Yes, it is difficult but we must learn to forgive so that our heavenly father will forgive our sins. We must let go for there is nothing we can do about the past, all what we have is the now moment. The future is even unknown, so let's try to make good use of it by being loving and kind to one another. *Mark 11:25 says: And when you stand praying, if you hold anything against anyone, forgive him so that your father in heaven may forgive your sins.* We often hold some grudges against our partners, families, friends, relatives and those around us and sometimes we feel justified and we are not willing to let go. When you are in Christ, there is no justification for a person's behavior. Separate the action from the person and let it go. It is healing to forgive each other so that we have love in our hearts which is the greatest commandment that God gave and see whether God will not move on your behalf.

James 5:16 says "Therefore confess your sins to each other so that you may be healed". Healing here refers to being made whole. He continues to say that the prayer of the righteous is powerful and effective. 1 john 3; 21 says *if our hearts do not condemn us, we have confidence in God and receive from him anything we ask because we keep his commands and do what pleases him.*

DO NOT BE SIN CONSCIOUS

Being conscious of sin can prevent you from entering the throne room of grace. You can stand between your true self and God. Your guilt and sin can stand between you entering into the throne room .Try and Let go of your sins and past regrets for God doesn't punish sin on earth. 2 Corinthians 5:17- 19 says that *"therefore if anyone is in Christ, he is a new creation; the old has gone, the new has come! All this is from God, who reconciled us to himself through Christ and gave us the ministry of reconciliation: that God was reconciling the world to Himself in Christ, not counting men's sins against them. And He has committed to us the message of reconciliation.* We suffer the consequences of sin we have brought upon ourselves. If He does what did Jesus Christ came to do? Punishing sin is in the old covenant not in the new covenant. *By calling this covenant "new," He has made the first one obsolete; and what is obsolete and outdated will soon disappear. (Hebrews 8:13).* In Christ, there is liberty not slavery if you only believe; Jesus Christ came to die for our sins. He is sitting at the right hand of the father interceding for us day in day out. Romans 6:1 caution us by saying that *what shall we say, then? Shall we go on sinning so that grace may increase?* As you are falling just lift your hand to God and He will lift you up. You don't intentionally go to sin because Christ has died for us, then you are making a mockery of the whole crucifixion and taking the grace for granted. *If we deliberately keep on sinning after we have received the knowledge of the truth, no sacrifice for sins is left, but only a fearful expectation of judgment and of raging fire that will consume the enemies of God.* (Hebrews 10: 26-27).Hebrews 2; 14-18 says *"since the children have flesh and blood, He too shared in their humanity so that by His death He might break the power of him who holds the power of death-that is the devil and free those who all their lives were held in slavery by their fear of death. For surely it is not angels He helps but Abraham's descendants. For this reason He had to be made like them, fully human in every way in order that He might become merciful and faithful high priest in service to God, and that He might make atonement for the sins of the people. Because He himself suffered when He was tempted, He is able to help those who are being tempted."* Feeling guilty of your sin will not let you enter the throne room. Your hope in Christ will intervene for you and your good deeds will intercede for you. Paul an Apostle of God who has always been eulogized was also perplexed in Christ, but never lost hope. If you are a Christian, you can be dumbfounded in a situation. As a matter of fact, you are not super human just try not to lose hope, your perplexity is to know Christ. In Hebrews 10:36-37 reads *you need to persevere so that when you have done the will of God, you will receive what he has promised. For, "In just a little while, he who is coming will come and will not delay."*

A pastor friend of mine, who was separated from his wife of fifteen years suddenly, had the desire for a young widow. He knew it wasn't right but his desire was so intense that he didn't heed to any advice. He fell for this young widow and the inevitable happened: The lady got pregnant for him. That was when he begun to realize where his desire has led him to. He became so guilty of this sin that it was drawing him farther away from God. He couldn't worship God anymore. The more he tried, the guiltier he became. He couldn't feel God's presence. It seemed as if the Holy Spirit was on vacation.

The lady started giving him attitude, nothing he did could please the woman. He felt helpless and said quietly to himself, let me rescind to my fate for I brought it upon myself. After visiting the young widow one hot afternoon, he boarded a bus at the local bus station to go back home. As he sat in the bus he couldn't help crying. He was so overwhelmed. He needed God; he couldn't get out of this hole alone. As he kept on thinking, He fell into a deep sleep. The scripture 1 Corinthians 10:13 appeared in a vision, *that no temptation has overtaken you except what is common to mankind. And God is faithful; He will not let you be tempted beyond what you can bear. But when you are tempted, He will also provide a way out so that you can endure it*. God says there is a way out, just cling to him. It will not be a cul-de-sac after all if He is in the picture.

Furthermore, a man I knew had cheated on his wife and was going through a divorce. He was so hard on himself because he knew it was his fault that the marriage was breaking down. He took full responsibility for his actions and apologized numerous times to his wife but the wife was very disappointed and could not trust him any longer. To his wife, the marriage was over. The man wanted a second chance at his marriage. I told him, if you are truly sorry, there is someone who can absorb your cross, so take your cross and follow Him. He invited God in the situation and allowed Him to have the final say. The wife went on with the divorce and it was granted. They all went on to live normal separate lives. After three years of living separately, the wife realized she had made a mistake and they reconciled and remarried. The man bore his cross that is the divorce and loneliness he went through for three years. Christ made it bearable so he was able to withstand it. Finally there was glory at the end when Christ absorbed his cross. We may be going through certain misfortunes at some point in our lives; Christ will always help us through it so that His glory will be manifested in the end.

Luke 14:27 says "And whosoever doth not bear his cross, and come after me, cannot be my disciple". You are worthy and your sins are not against you, if you fully open your arms wide and embrace the cross.

ENTERING THE THRONE ROOM OF GRACE

James 5:11 says *"As you know, we count as blessed those who have persevered. You have heard of Job's perseverance and have seen what the lord finally brought about".* The lord is full of compassion and mercy. Persevering in the midst of adversaries and having patience will enable you enter the throne room of grace. Hebrews 4:16 sums it all up by saying that *"let us then approach God's throne of grace with confidence, so that we may receive mercy and find grace to help us in our time of need"* God knows best, it is His wish that will prevail. The lord is full of compassion and mercy, Christ in you, the hope of glory. God has to remove all the dead parts of the tree that is not allowing the tree to be fruitful. When the dead parts are being removed from a tree, it feels a lot of discomfort. So when we are being pruned, it's difficult but it is the only way to be more fruitful and you will be glad He did. It is as hard as it is beautiful when you finally embrace Christ. The intensity of the suffering and difficulty is the same as the glory that will come along. Romans 8:17 says *"Now if we are children, then we are heirs-heirs of God and co-heirs with Christ, if indeed we share in His sufferings in order that we may also share in His glory".* I remember my childhood years when I used to play the see saw game; it was one game I really enjoyed. When one side goes up the other side goes down. I am going to relate this game to having Christ in your life. When Christ in your life goes up things of the flesh goes down so that *you are transformed by the renewal of your mind so that you don't conform to this world and you may prove what the will of God is, that which is acceptable and perfect (Romans 12:2)*

Furthermore, when we are strengthened in Christ the goal is to make Him our only consolation. We pass through many "trials" or I would like to call it "strengtheners". In 2 Corinthians 4; 16-17 Paul said *"therefore we do not lose heart. Even though our outward man is perishing yet the inward man is being renewed day by day. For our light affliction, is but for a moment, is working for us a far more exceeding and eternal weight of glory".*

When you are going through such trials or strengtheners, I urge you to press on; you are closer to Christ than you think. When Christ becomes your All in All, your faith in God grows and you call things of the flesh vanity. As Paul said in Philippians 4:7-10 "***But what things were gain to me, these I have counted loss for Christ. Yet indeed I also count all things loss for the excellence of the knowledge of Christ Jesus my Lord, for whom I have suffered the loss of all things, and count them as rubbish, that I may gain Christ and be found in Him, not having my own righteousness which is from the law, but that which is through faith in Christ, the righteousness which is from God by faith; that I may know Him and the power of His resurrection and the fellowship of His sufferings, being conformed to His death. If by any means, I may attain to the resurrection from the dead"***. When you totally find Christ, you put off your former self and embrace your true self. In Ephesians 4:20-24 it says "***But you have not so learned Christ, if indeed you have heard him and have been taught by him as the truth is in Jesus: that you put off, concerning your former conduct, the old man which grows corrupt according to the deceitful lusts, and be renewed in the spirit of your mind, and that you put on the new man which was created according to God, in true righteousness and holiness"***.

CHAPTER TWO
THE GENESIS OF PRAYER
THE FIRST COMMUNICATION BETWEEN GOD AND MAN

God created us in his own image and God blessed us and said "Be fruitful and increase" (Genesis 1:27-28) everything that we ever wanted was given to us.

First, man was without sin therefore God could talk audibly to man anytime he wanted, there was no barrier.

God's first one way talk with man can be found in Genesis 2; 16 -17 which was an instruction. "And the Lord God commanded man, you are free to eat from any tree in the garden; but you must not eat from the tree of the knowledge of good and evil, for when you eat from it you will certainly die."

The first dialogue between God and man found in the bible was initiated by God and it can be found in Genesis 3:8-12 when Adam and Eve fell by eating from the forbidden tree. Then the man and his wife heard the sound of Lord God as he was walking in the garden in the cool of the day, and they hid from the Lord God among the trees of the garden. But the Lord God called to the man, where are you? He answered, I heard you in the garden and I was afraid because I was naked and so I hid. And He said, who told you that you were naked? Have you eaten from the tree that I commanded you not to eat from? The man said, "The woman you put here with me-she gave me some fruit from the tree, and I ate it" note that Man was in the presence of God when the communication was being done. Prayer needs to be in the presence of God for it to be effective. Being in the presence of God means focusing on Him when you pray to make the atmosphere fully charged with the Holy Spirit, which can only happen when you are praying through Christ.

AFTER THE FALL

After the fall, God said, Man has become like one of us knowing good and evil in Genesis 3:22. It is well noted in the bible that God and Man were still communicating after the fall. In Genesis 4:6-9 God initiated a talk with Cain. We could see that God initiating the communication with man was a normal thing that happened in the past.

It is also made clear here that *for communication to be effective we need to be in the Lord's presence*. Afterwards people begun to call on the name of the lord which can be found in Genesis 4:25

GOD LOOKED AT THE HEART

In Genesis 6:5 *the lord saw how great the wickedness of the human race had become on earth and that every inclination of the thoughts of the human heart was only evil at that time*.

Now, thoughts are prayers. Their minds were filled with evil. See the way the heart was so important to God. Although they were not vocal about their wicked intentions God knew and took notice of the wickedness in their hearts. The evil prayers in their heart at that time made God regret his decision by making man on earth.

In Genesis 6: 5-7 we realize that our prayers can make God angry.

The prayer that God recognized was prayer from the hearts of people, even though not said but was in their minds.

"But the things that come out of a person's mouth come from the heart, and these defile them. For out of the heart come evil thoughts—murder, adultery, sexual immorality, theft, false testimony, slander. These are what defile a person; but eating with unwashed hands does not defile them." (Matthew 15: 18-20).

Noah was a man who found favour with God. Why did Noah find favour with God? Noah had a faithful heart and was righteous.

Because of Noah's faithfulness, the lord established a covenant with him. He said, never again will all life be destroyed. (Genesis 9:8). It is well established that the heart is very important to God and the heart speaks volumes. When you are communicating with your heart or only your lips the omnipotent one knows and He will only recognize a heartfelt prayer.

In Proverbs 15:11 it reads "hell and destruction are before the Lord; so how much more the hearts of the sons of men".

WHAT IS PRAYER

Life can be overwhelming and we can be overtaken by events. We want a change! We pray all manner of prayers and forget the heart but the heart is the determinant of whether our prayers are answered or not. Ephesians 6:18 says *"And pray in the spirit on all occasions with all kinds of prayers and requests. With this in mind, be alert and always keep on praying for all the Lord's people." Prayer is a heartfelt communication between you and your maker.* If the communication doesn't flow from your heart it is not a genuine prayer.

How lord or soft your voice is or how short or long does not count. *Prayer flows from the genuineness of your heart.* Many at times we believe that the louder our requests are, the quicker your prayer is answered, which is not so.

Prayer is not burdened and it is not associated with any rituals. Prayer is like talking to your best buddy who you know has unconditional love for you, so therefore you will come to him or her in your true self. You do not present yourself superficially owing to the fact that the relationship is so mutual and so personal. Prayer is a form of sacrifice; Sacrifice is a form of worship. Romans 12:1 says *"therefore I urge you, brothers and sisters, in view of God's mercy, to offer your bodies as a living sacrifice, holy and pleasing to God-this is your true and proper worship".* You can't offer your bodies as true and proper worship without having an interpersonal relationship with your maker. In John 4:24 it says that those who worship him, worship him in spirit and in truth. ***It is the sincerity of your words in prayer that counts to God.***

JESUS IS THE MASTER CLEANER

We should also note that the relationship between us and God is like a Daddy-child relationship. Even in our sins we should be able to come to God in Prayer and commune with Him. Just like a baby with soiled pants sits on her mother's lap and her mother allows it with so much joy that is even less of how God loves us even when we think we are unclean. At times, we are in a very worse situation, nothing seems to work. We feel destroyed. We are ashamed of ourselves. Where we have gotten to in life, we feel there is no achievement. We suddenly ask ourselves, what is my purpose on earth? At this age, I should have been this or that. Life is meaningless. One man I knew was in his early fifty's, and had three young children, he felt helpless. He was working but his salary was meager compared to his responsibilities. He couldn't foot his bills and fending for his family was a big issue. In short, he was struggling. He felt he was in a very big mess. And he was? But no mess is greater than the Master cleaner who cleans to perfection and leaves no trace of dirt even if you use a magnifying glass. He tried to clean the mess himself and he wasn't successful, Call the Master Cleaner, I said. He said I can't afford it? I said this Master Cleaner cleans for free. He just needs your heart. Are you really serious he asked? Yes he does, I replied. What am I waiting for? He asked further. He gave his life to Jesus and he received rest which was unimaginable. Have you created a mess of yourselves and you feel you are so dirty? All cleaning agents are not working, the stain is still there. You cannot do it yourself; the only person who can clean that mess is Jesus. He is the Master cleaner. He cleans without any trace of dirt and leaves you so sparkling clean. Jesus always takes the dejected, the tattered, the destroyed and He makes it whole. You will live a fulfilled life and you will receive the peace of God through starting a personal relationship with our Lord and Saviour.

TURN YOUR SHAME INTO A NAME

You have done wrong things in the past and everyone thinks you are a bad person. You made a mistake and you cannot let go of that past and you feel so ashamed. There are issues in life, which are weighing you down. You do not understand why you are not getting pregnant after ten years of marriage. Has the good Lord that you serve left you barren? The promotion at work that will lead you to your big financial break is not forthcoming, you begin to wonder why.

When you are ashamed of your past or worried about your unknown future that is when you can find God. In that moment, where nothing seems to work for you, you sit in a quiet mood most often. It is in that quietness, that you can hear the spirit of God which is gentle and true.

When we cling to God through those trying moments, we find our purpose in life. Paul said in 2 Corinthians 12:9, but he said to me, *"My grace is sufficient for you, for my power is made perfect in weakness."* Therefore I will boast all the more gladly about my weaknesses, so that Christ's power may rest on me.

We are all uniquely created and our journeys may be different. One thing for sure, we are all partakers of God's grace, if we let ourselves go and let God in. Then Jesus said to his disciples, *"Whoever wants to be my disciple must deny themselves and take up their cross and follow me. For whoever wants to save their life will lose it, but whoever loses their life for me will find it"*. (Matthew 16:24-25). Jesus has already taken your shame and pain away by nailing it on the cross. When you embrace the cross, He gives you a new identity. You are now a new creation, old things have become new. You begin to live the life that God predestined for you to live.

MOTIVE BEHIND YOUR PRAYER

Another point that is most neglected is the motive behind one's prayer. In James 4:3 says *"yet you do not have because you do not ask, you ask and do not receive, because you ask amiss, that you may spend it on your pleasures"*. I will narrate the story of Sika. Sika wanted to be a Lawyer at all cost, she had a very good analytical mind and neighbours always came to her with marital problems, work related problems and other family issues which she solved amicably. Everybody advised her to do law for she will be a great Lawyer. Secretly, Sika had a problem she was being laud over by her husband and she felt her independence was taken away. Her husband worked at the local radio station where his salary was meager and they lived on a low budget. She felt that if she goes to law school to become a lawyer, then her husband and she could run shoulders. So she applied for and gained admission to do law in one of the public universities in the country. How to pay the school fees had suddenly become a problem. She prayed to God, but it looks as if her prayers were not heard. Her husband tried securing a loan to help her start the law degree but all was to no avail. Why didn't God hear her prayer? She wanted this, to be a lawyer was her greatest dream and unfortunately it wasn't realized. She tried to secure money to pay for the law degree herself, but it proved futile. Very disappointed, she finally gave up. Years passed by and she had totally forgotten about that law degree. Her attitude toward her husband changed. She found a job as an assistant sales girl in a grocery shop. She worked tirelessly and supported her husband to raise two kids. Their home was a lovely home full of happiness. One night, Sika was watching a documentary on TV on how innocent people were jailed and some could not afford a Lawyer. Amy cried, oh how I wish I was a lawyer God, I would have helped this innocent people for free. A few weeks later she saw an advert of law school admissions of a prestigious university. She applied and the long and short of it all is that she gained admission with full scholarship. Sika and her husband rejoiced and sang the song "How great thou art". It was a joyous moment. The first time she wanted to be a Lawyer, her motive was totally wrong so her prayer was not answered.

BELIEVE IN YOUR PRAYER

Furthermore, when we ask, we must believe and not doubt or have contentions in our minds and be unified in the spirit; James addresses doubters like the sea waves which are so unstable. There was a young woman who had a sick child, she had prayed for the child to be healed but she always had it at the back of her mind that her child will die. The inevitable happened, her child died. Let's try to believe in the prayer that we have said to God.

WHO SHOULD PRAY

1Timothy 2:1 says I urge, then, first of all, that petitions, prayers, intercession and thanksgiving be made for all people. *Prayer is therefore for all persons.*

I am young, why should I pray all the time, I have a lot of life ahead of me. I will wait till when I am 50 then I will be prayerful. But in *Ecclesiastes 12;1 we are told to remember our creator in the days of our youth, before the days of trouble come and the years approach when you will say, I find no pleasure in them.*

Daniel in his youth also was a strong man of prayer who set an example and his king Nebucchadnezzar decided to follow the God he served.

King Hezekiah was an example of an old king who prayed to God. He was an old ruler but he was humble enough to pray to God.

Samuel as a little boy prayed and heard from God. Everyone can have access to God; you just have to submit yourselves to prayer.

TYPES OF PRAYER

There are two main types of prayer
Personal prayer (Praying for oneself)
Intercessory prayer (Praying for others)

PERSONAL PRAYER

In the book of Matthew, Jesus taught us how to pray personal prayers. He said and I quote from chapter 6:6-8. *But when you pray, go into your room, close the door and pray to your father, who is unseen. Then your father, who sees what is done in secret, will reward you. And when you pray, do not keep on babbling like pagans, for they think they will be heard because of their many words. Do not be like them, for your father knows what you need before you ask him.*

INTERCESSORY PRAYER

We are taught not to be discriminatory when praying for people as followers of Christ. We should pray for people irrespective of religion, race, colour, gender and whether they are our enemies or friends.

Jesus also encouraged us to pray for all including our enemies. *He said, But I tell you, love your enemies and pray for those who persecute you.* (Matthew 5:44).

CHAPTER THREE
HOW TO PRAY
PERSONAL PRAYER (PRAYING FOR ONESELF)
TAKE EVERYTHING TO GOD IN PRAYER

Whilst studying for my PhD degree, I had an assignment to submit and the deadline was approaching. I needed to read a book to be able to do the assignment. My funds were so low so I could not buy the book. Hey! I had an alternative, I was going to surf the net whether I could get a free copy to download. I searched fruitlessly! I could not get it. Then, I remembered I had a father in heaven. So I decided to tell my father about it in prayer. The next day, I lay on the couch in the hall. "Something" prompted me to search the book on my phone again. The first search I did, there it was, and how it got there I have no idea. Finally, I could do my assignment. The lyrics of the song "What a friend we have in Jesus" written by Joseph M. Scriven and composed by Charles Crozart Converse makes more meaning to me now. What a friend we have in Jesus,

All our sins and griefs to bear,
What a privilege to carry,
Everything to God in prayer,
Oh what peace we often forfeit,

Oh what needless pain we bear,
All because we do not carry
Everything to God in Prayer.

When we do not carry EVERYTHING TO GOD IN PRAYER, WE BEAR NEEDLESS PAIN and we do not have peace.

A SAMPLE PRAYER JESUS TAUGHT

The Lord's Prayer (Matthew 6:9-13) this is then how you should pray;

> ***"Our father in heaven,***
> ***Hallowed be your name,***
> ***Your kingdom come,***
> ***Your will be done,***
> ***On earth as it is in heaven.***
> ***Give us today our daily bread.***
> ***And forgive us our debts,***
> ***As we also have forgiven our debtors.***
> ***And lead us not into temptation,***
> ***But deliver us from the evil one.***

The Lord's Prayer is a summary of Christ's teaching. God is acknowledged as the most sacred one from the beginning. In the beginning was the Word, and the Word was with God, and the Word was God. (John 1:1)

Then, it tells us to pray according to the will of God in whatever situation we may find ourselves in. whatever He planned from the beginning must be fulfilled on earth. In short, He fulfills destinies according to His will. After that we are told to ask for our daily bread. Ask God only for what you need today not tomorrow, for tomorrow has enough troubles of its own. Matthew 6:34 sums it all up by saying that ***"therefore do not worry about tomorrow, for tomorrow will worry about itself. Each day has enough trouble of its own".*** He asked us to be forgiving and have love in our hearts irrespective of whatever we may be going through. When we are able to forgive others of any wrong doing then He will be able to forgive us our sins too. It works hand in hand. Furthermore, when you hold on to Christ, He will always lead you out of temptation. The temptations will come alright but there will be a way out of you, only if you give Him the chance to lead you. No temptation[a] has overtaken you except what is common to mankind. And God is faithful; he will not let you be tempted beyond what you can bear. But when you are tempted, he will also provide a way out so that you can endure it.(1 Corinthians 10:13) He will deliver us from all evil, meaning we are of the world but we are not supposed to live according to the world when we profess Christ in our hearts. I have given them your word and the world has hated them, for they are not of the world any more than I am of the world. *My prayer is not that you take them out of the world but that you protect them from the evil one.* (John 17: 14-15)Are we ready to let ourselves go for God's kingdom to take over our lives? Once, on being asked by the Pharisees when the kingdom of God would come, Jesus replied, "The coming of the kingdom of God is not something that can be observed, nor will people say, 'Here it is,' or 'there it is,' because the kingdom of God is in your midst. (John 17: 20-21)" By praying thy kingdom come in the Lord's Prayer we are ready to submit ourselves to the Holy Spirit, by giving up our will for His will to be made perfect in our lives. Ephesians 6: 12 say that; for our struggle is not against flesh and blood, but against the rulers, against the authorities, against the powers of this dark world and against the spiritual forces of evil in the heavenly realms. Even though there are other rulers, we should submit to the Holy Spirit for God to rule over our lives. Finally it is noted that the power and glory that surpasses all is in God's kingdom always.

ADVANTAGES OF PERSONAL PRAYER

- Personal prayer helps one to have an encounter with God at his or her own time with no influences at all.
- Your prayer tend to be concise and straight to the point
- You lay your requests before God
- The probability of you praying a true prayer is high.
- You easily focus on what you want to pray about.

DISADVANTAGES OF PERSONAL PRAYER

- You can be discouraged

- You can be lonely and so bored
- It could be stressful
- Your interest could be waned.
- Sometimes, you are lost for words when the situation is overwhelming

GROUP PRAYER

Now, group praying is the trend these days, the group members look up to the leader for prayer topics and all members of the group pray along. In Africa, it has suddenly become the" in thing" and the easy way out to escape any challenge one may be faced in life. Unfortunately, individual prayers and direct relationship with God has been overlooked. Everyone wants a faster way for his or her prayers to be answered and thinks group praying is the answer, although the benefits of praying in groups cannot be overlooked.

ADVANTAGES OF GROUP PRAYER

- It encourages other members to pray when they feel they are weak.
- It also serves as a motivator when you are working towards a common goal.
- You get the benefit of good teaching from the bible when members are conversant with the bible and have the Holy Spirit.

There were group prayers in the bible In Acts 2; 42 believers devoted themselves to the apostle's teaching and to fellowship and to the breaking of bread and to prayer. In Acts chapter 12, Peter was released from prison miraculously by an angel when he went to sleep. Owing to the fact that constant prayer was offered to God by the church for him. In verse 6 to 7 it says "and when Herod was about to bring him out, that night Peter was sleeping, bound with two chains between two soldiers; and the guards before the door were keeping the prison. Now, behold, an angel of the Lord stood by him and a light shone in the prison; and he stuck Peter on the side and raised him up, saying Arise quickly!" And his chains fell off his hands. Peter thought he had seen a vision but it was so real. An angel of the Lord was sent to the rescue when group prayers were said for Peter in prison. In Acts 16 when Paul and Silas were praying and singing hymns to God at midnight, there was a sudden earthquake that it shook the foundations of the prison and immediately all the doors were opened and everyone's chains were loosed. The power of group prayer therefore cannot be underestimated.

DISADVANTAGES OF GROUP PRAYER
- You can't pray your own prayers
- It is time consuming.
- Your focus is shifted to the focus of the group
- Your participation can be limited
- Conflict arises owing to the fact that every individual has different needs.

When praying in groups, it's not about babbling words or repeating what the leader says, learn to pray according to your heart and be under the guidance of the Holy Spirit.

SUBMITTING TO THE HOLY SPIRIT

Prayer must be done in the presence of the Holy Spirit for it to be effective whether one is praying individually or in a group. The Holy Spirit is the only guide that we need. When Jesus Christ ascended into heaven, he left us the Holy Spirit who is our helper in all things. John 14;26 reads *"But the advocate, the holy spirit, whom the father will send in my name, will teach you all things and remind you of everything I have said to you.* Have a heart that submits to the Holy Spirit and He will guide you. Living according to the Spirit makes life fulfilling. Often than not, we tend to take control of our own lives but our lives belong to God, In Jeremiah 29;11 the Lord declared that "I *know the plans I have for you, a plan to prosper you and not to harm you, Plans to give you a hope and a future.* We have a great helper that is the Holy Spirit; we don't have to be great at praying. Romans 8:14 says *"For those who are led by the spirit of God are the children of God. The spirit you received does not make you slaves, so that you live in fear again: rather the spirit you received brought about your adoption to sonship. And by him we cry, "Abba, Father."*

One morning, I sat down on my best couch thinking of what my family will eat the next day. The message " do not be anxious about anything, but in every situation, by prayer and petition, with thanksgiving, present your requests to God, and the peace of God which transcends all understanding will guard your hearts and your minds in Christ Jesus" (Philippians 4: 6-7) came echoing in my mind. I knew it was the Lord speaking to me. I humbly said a prayer to God to meet my need. I texted a colleague of mine later on to check on how she was doing. She replied with a call and we talked about other issues but not financial issues. After the call ended, I decided to check my phone. To my utter surprise, she has sent me money. I was shocked! Has my prayer been answered just like that? Then I realized, I was led by the spirit to call her. Most times we want something that is not forthcoming because we are not asking God and interacting with His spirit who is always around us. By so doing we worry unnecessarily. Matthew 6:34 reads *"Therefore do not worry about tomorrow, for tomorrow will worry about itself. Each day has enough trouble of its own".*

A young man was on his way to visit a sick brother. He sat in a bus quietly wondering what was making his brother's sickness get worse. His mind was full of many disturbing thoughts. Unexpectedly, he heard the spirit telling him to preach about forgiveness. He looked around and found some young girls giggling in the bus. He thought to himself, if I start preaching those girls are going to make fun of me. So he decided not to do it. The spirit kept prompting him, and then he finally said to himself: this is certainly not the time. An appropriate time will come for this message. The Holy Spirit was therefore ignored. In the middle of the journey, the bus stopped and a lady got down furiously and he automatically knew the message was to that lady. He felt so bad after but the opportunity was gone. Two weeks after, he was going to visit a friend when he saw an obituary of the lady who got off the bus with so much anger. He wept! He kept on asking people around if they knew the lady who was on the obituary. One middle aged woman told him of how the young lady had stabbed his irresponsible husband and the husband had stabbed him in return. What happened he asked curiously? The lady caught the husband red-handed having an affair with another woman. When did this happen he inquired further? The woman replied; two weeks ago, sadly the deceased knew nothing about forgiveness she added. The young man bowed his head in shame. He realized that because he did not obey the spirit to preach forgiveness, a beautiful soul has been lost. ***Luke 11:13 says if you then, though you are evil, know how to give good gifts to your children, how much more will your father in heaven give the Holy spirit to those who ask him.***

The Holy Spirit is the still small voice you hear in your quiet moment. It is a gentle spirit and one of the best gifts you could ever have. You need to interact with the Holy Spirit to live a fulfilling life.

Jesus himself was led by the spirit to pray fast and pray for forty days and night. Furthermore, the Holy Spirit guides us in so many ways when we pray.

I once wanted a Nanny owing to the fact that I was struggling to take care of three kids below the age of six. It was so hard, hey! I am no superwoman, I needed help. So I started scouting for help, I searched in all places but I couldn't find. I hadn't even thought to pray. Should I also pray about this? I asked myself? I finally said a word of prayer. A few weeks after, my husband brought home someone and said Honey, I brought you a nanny. I was so surprised! Has God answered my prayer so soon? Wow! What a wonderful God? I should have prayed earlier, I said quietly. All of a sudden, I started feeling uneasy about the nanny. When I introduced my kids to the Nanny, they all left with a sullen face. Then I pulled my husband aside and said; I don't feel comfortable about this and the kids are not happy. Why he asked angrily? You needed a Nanny and I have brought you one. Yes, I appreciate your effort but unfortunately, I do not feel this is the one. So he agreed to send the Nanny away reluctantly, of course. A few weeks after, he called me and said, honey you were right about the Nanny. The Nanny went to live with a couple down the street and she maltreated their kids so badly. I smiled and said, thank you Holy Spirit. After I said a word of prayer, God sent me the Holy Spirit to help me in my decision and that was the sudden discomfort I felt which didn't allow me to employ the Nanny. We hugged each other and we just couldn't thank God enough for all his goodness and mercy. Sometimes we ask ourselves whether God is alive! Based on the circumstances we find ourselves. We cannot pray and our faith is challenged. I remember when I was looking for a job without success. I had prayed all manner of prayers to no avail. So I complained to a friend. Then he said, turn all your complaints and worries into prayers. Then I said, I cannot pray! Can't you understand? Then he said, tell God, you cannot pray that is prayer from a pure heart. Tell God exactly how you feel. Now what is prayer? Prayer is a heartfelt communication between you and your maker. Anything you feel, you tell God as it is. Put all the prayer methodologies aside and pray from a genuine heart. You don't have to be great at praying. If you cannot pray, tell God so! The Holy Spirit always intercedes for us; He is our great helper in all things. Don't try and force words out of your mouth when in fact you do not have anything to say. He hears all our words and even our thoughts and recognizes them when it is from a pure heart. After praying heartfelt prayers, God heard me! Yes He did! He gave me the most wonderful job ever in His own time.

"Likewise the Spirit also helps in our weaknesses. For we do not know what we should pray for as we ought, but the Spirit Himself makes intercession for us with groanings which cannot be uttered. Now He who searches the hearts, knows what the mind of the Spirit is, because He makes intercessions for the saints according to the will of God". (Romans 8:26-27)

PLACES TO PRAY

There are instances in the bible that prayer was done at the riverside, on the mountain top; in a solitary place and in synagogues .You can pray anywhere as long as you pray in the spirit owing to the fact that God is everywhere and that place becomes sanctified immediately you start praying. Prayer is not limited to the church building, you could pray in your office, whilst cooking dinner or whilst taking a bath. It is actually your heart that God wants.

Prayer can be done in a variety of ways. It could be a song, recitals, words that can be said silently or loudly. We could also pray in whatever posture we feel comfortable in. whether we sit, stand, kneel, lie flat or we lift our hands up, all that matters to God is our heart. ***Let your worship be the out pouring of your relationship with Christ Jesus.***

CHAPTER FOUR
WHEN TO PRAY?

Prayer is timeless and the most essential spiritual exercise we can all engage in, which is fruitful. There is no time limit to prayer. There is absolutely no time frame for prayer. Most at times we pray when we are faced with a dark situation, it will do us a lot of good if we pray when we are so free and not stressed out. In spite of our daily hassles we often feel we do not have time to pray and we pray only when there is a problem.

Praying when things are going on smoothly always keeps you at peace when the challenges arrive. Most of the time we feel we do not have time to pray and we suddenly have excuses like Oh I am getting late for work, the house chores are weighing me down, I have to send the kids to school. The last thing I really want to do is to pray. Begin your day with prayer, just spare a minute or two to talk to God, it really helps and it puts you in a positive mood and ignites the confidence in us. Daniel prayed many times a day although he worked for the government. In his busy schedule, he found time for God to commune with Him.

The bible tells us *to pray without ceasing* in 1 Thessalonians 5:17 we are encouraged to pray continually which means there is no set time to pray. We should pray at all times from the heart wherever we find ourselves in whatever situation. For Prayer is a great ingredient for a delicious meal. There is no benchmark in prayer, just make sure it is a heartfelt one.

I will tell the story of a man who suddenly had the urge to pray. He started praying and wanted to stop along the line to do other stuff, but he could not. The Holy Spirit was encouraging him to pray more. After he finally stopped, he realized that he has been praying for three hours. This was a man who could not even pray for 5 minutes. Just as he heaved a sigh of relief, the phone rang. He responded and his son in law was at the other end and he said your daughter just gave birth to a baby boy. The last three hours was so critical, we thought we were going to lose her. The baby was breeched but miraculously the baby turned into a cephalous (head down) position. Wow! The man started singing songs of praise. He now understood why he could not stop praying in the last three hours. The Holy Spirit was urging him on to pray for three hours.

Prayer could also be spontaneous; I would like to relate this to a friend of mine whose son had asphyxia. The Doctors tried all they could but they could not get the boy to breathe normally. His breathing was getting worse. The boy was dying. Suddenly, the Doctor said, let's pray! So, all the doctors and nurses in the room started praying. It was like a mini church service in a hospital. Suddenly, the boy gasped for breath and he started breathing normally. The boy was healed unexpectedly.

Prayer could also be persistent, Luke 18:1-8) Jesus told the story of the persistent widow who defied all odds and had her request granted because of her persistence even though the judge was wicked, how much more our heavenly father who loves us unconditionally.

An event occurred in my home, my 7 year old daughter's tooth came out one day. Then she said, mummy, I am going to put this tooth under my pillow for the tooth fairy to visit and give me money. Then I said, ok go ahead. Apparently, I was so broke that I totally forgot. The next morning she said sadly, mummy the tooth fairy didn't come. Then I remembered I should have put the money under the pillow. It went on for three days continuously, there was no sign of the tooth fairy and her brother had started discouraging her that there was nothing like the tooth fairy, she kept on believing that somehow the tooth fairy will come. Unfortunately, the tooth fairy was so broke. But she never gave up she kept on putting the tooth under her pillow. Then I got up and asked my husband can you spare me some money then he said, why not. What are you going to do with it he asked; I am going to put it under my daughter's pillow. Then he laughed heartily. Then I said, I feel her anxiety, I just want to do it for her so she can be happy. So my daughter got up the next morning and was happy. She ran into the kitchen where I was making breakfast. Mummy! The tooth fairy came and she gave me a big hug. The tooth fairy didn't forget about me, I knew she will come. Then the doubting Thomas that is her brother was like, mummy why didn't the tooth fairy come when I lost a tooth, and then the sister replied because you didn't believe in the tooth fairy.

Now, even I being an earthly mother suddenly felt the frustration of my daughter and I wanted to fulfill that dream for her at all cost. How much more our heavenly father who loves us. When praying with a persistent heart we should always believe in the fact that our heavenly father will come through for us. God always comes through for those who believe in him. ***Mark 11:24 says therefore I tell you, whatever you ask for in prayer, believe that you have received it and it will be yours.***

THE PURPOSE OF PRAYER
WHY DO WE PRAY

God loves us so much that He wants us to talk to Him all the time. We all have equal access to God because we are His children. We can all benefit a close relationship by opening our hearts to Him, so that He will walk us through the journey of life.

If you don't open up to your best friend, he/she will not know what the situation really is, to help you. I had a friend, whom we shared everything. It got to a time; I felt this friend was being judgmental so I started hiding some stuff from her. I then projected myself as if everything was alright. Truth be told, I was suffering inside. Anytime, she asked me whether I was okay, I hurriedly replied, yes. I then got tired of hiding information from her. One day, I broke down and told her the whole situation. She quickly said, why didn't you tell me all this? I just couldn't tell you, I replied. Okay, she continued I have the exact help you need. My friend helped me in a way that I could have never imagined. I felt so much happier and relieved. Best of all, my problem was solved and the relationship was even better. This is exactly, how God wants us to come to Him in Prayer. When you are truthful to Him, He hears you and comes to your aid and best of all your relationship with Him is strengthened. Let us not present ourselves superficially to Him. Let's come as we are, so that He will give us the needed help and we get even closer to Him.

God is spirit, and his worshipers must worship in the Spirit and in truth." John 4:24

THE BUMPY RIDE

A woman asked her husband to buy her a second hand car. The husband said to her Anne, I will buy you the car but be patient. Anne became very disobedient to her husband because of her husband's inability to buy her a car. She grew distant from her husband. A car was tearing their marriage apart. The nagging and the insults worsened. Home has turned into hell for the husband. The relationship was deteriorating. The husband was gradually been pushed out. After a while, the wife came home one day and saw a beautiful car parked in the yard of their house. It was a very beautiful and an expensive brand new car. Wow! She exclaimed. What important visitor do we have here? She went close to the Car and found a note in the windscreen. She opened the note and she started crying. She cried her eyes out.

The note read" Honey, I have finally been able to buy you the car. I was waiting for the right time to give you this car. I was able to find out one thing; you cherished the car more than me. You do not value the relationship but you value only the things you want to have. Have your car and enjoy your new relationship! See my lawyer, until then, enjoy the ride!" Are we interested in having a relationship with God or we are interested in prayer because of the products we expect to get? If we are patient and we build this relationship, we even get products we are not asking for. In these days, we want the product more than the relationship. Ask yourself: If I get the product will I continue to cherish that relationship? God wants us to have the relationship so that we trust him enough to only give us the best of things in life. Let's begin to cherish that relationship whether we have by products or not, so that we become God's friend. Prayer is the ultimate way to commune with God so that He will be your companion in life.

"Now unto Him, who is able to do exceedingly, abundantly, above all that you ask or think according to the power that works in us." Ephesians 3:20

Most of the times we tend to focus on the results not the change. The change is the prayer that should ultimately be your focus. Jeremiah 32:26-27 says then the word of the Lord came to Jeremiah*: I am the Lord, the God of all mankind. Is anything too hard for me?*

In the bible, all forms of Prayer were said for deliverance, protection, healing and among others. In these days we think Prayer can make us achieve our bucket list.

Prayer ultimately gives you an inner peace and rest that God is in control and it makes you rely on him recognizing the fact that He is your all sufficiency no matter what. When we pray, our hearts are molded because when Jesus enters the heart He changes the heart and takes all the negativities away. By our hearts changed it eventually turns our lives around and our minds are transformed to be more Christ like. Prayer also helps to build a strong relationship in Christ so that His grace will be with us always.

CHAPTER FIVE
A HEARTFELT PRAYER

Praying from your heart is a genuine prayer. Below are practical examples of prayers through the heart. ***Above all else, guard your heart, for everything you do flows from it. (Proverbs 4:23).***

A CONTRITE HEART

Prayer these days is like manual labour. We use so much of our physical strength. Come to God as you are, if you are broken come broken, don't work it. ***"For it is God, who works in you to will and to act in order to fulfill his good purpose. (Philipians 2:13)".***

In Psalm 51 verse 17 it is made clear that God loves a contrite spirit. ***He said these are the ones I look on with favour: those who are humble and contrite in spirit.*** These are examples of prayers that God answered that were based on a contrite heart. Before we move to the bible, a lady that I knew worked as a house keeper in a rich woman's house. The woman was so disrespectful to her and maltreated her but she continued working there as that was the only way she could make ends meet, noting the fact that she was coming from an impoverished background. A little misunderstanding occurred between her and her boss. The woman then relieved her of her duties and she was sent home. But where was home? That was the only place she felt was her home. She felt dejected and helpless. Then she remembered she had a God who could save her. She has been robbed of everything that she knew, her only hope was God. She went into her wooden structure, closed the door and wept like never before asking God to change her situation. She has suddenly become tired. After a few days she decided to sell bread for a friend she knew. She started hawking the bread on the street. Then she met a man who was a lay preacher who was supposed to travel to Canada but his travel documents were not going through. The man expressed interest in her; they prayed and rested despite the fact that the answer lies in God's hands. After two years of waiting, at God's own time, the man married the woman and they have started their Christian ministry in Canada.

A time back, I gave my curriculum vitae to a woman who was in a capacity to give me a job. She promised, she will call me immediately she got home. I waited and waited for six months for her call. I was getting frustrated and I was tired of waiting. So I knelt down on my knees helplessly and prayed to God. I acknowledged the fact that it was God who will help me and not her after all. A day after, I received a call from her, saying she never looked at my curriculum vitae until yesterday. She gave me a job offer which was a perfect fit for me. God indeed answered my prayer when I came to Him with a contrite heart.

JABEZ'S PRAYER

The prayer of Jabez has always inspired me. In 1 Chronicles 4; 9-10, we are told that Jabez was more honourable than his brothers. His mother had named him Jabez, saying, "I gave birth to him in pain" Jabez cried out to the God of Israel, oh that you would bless me and enlarge my territory! Let your hand be with me, and keep me from harm so that I will be free from pain" And God granted his request. Jabez's destiny was changed when he cried out to the lord and God granted his request. Detailing further, Jabez was born honourable but societal influences and pressures of the world changed his identity. ***God restored him only when he had come to God broken.***

HANNAH'S PRAYER

God himself closed the womb of Hannah but she still believed God could give her a son. In 1st Samuel 1:10. ***In her deep anguish Hannah prayed to the Lord, weeping bitterly.*** In verse 13 it was accounted that Hannah was praying from her heart and Eli thought she was drunk. In verse 15 Hannah replied "Not so, my lord. I am a woman who is deeply troubled. I have not been drinking wine and beer; I was pouring out my soul to the Lord. Hannah looked up to God only not even Eli. The first thing Hannah did was to pour out her soul before the promise and her promise was also from her heart and God gave her a son.

KING HEZEKIAH'S PRAYER

In 2 Kings 20 verse 1 the lord sent Amoz to tell Hezekiah he was going to die from his illness and that he should put his house in order. The lord had spoken and it was final but in verse 2 ***King Hezekiah turned his face to the wall and cried and recounted his works before God for God to change his decision.*** In the Old Testament works were a prerequisite for salvation but in the new covenant it is grace. The lord gave him more years to live because he came to God with a contrite spirit. He didn't even appeal to Amoz who was a mere mortal. He turned his face to the wall, meaning not looking at anyone but only God. How much more today when we don't even have to recount our works but believe in Christ. In John 6:28-29. They asked Him, what must we do to do the works God requires? Then Jesus answered "the work of God is this: to believe in the one he has sent." Where believing is to do what He says and let the grace work on our behalf.

Anthony was a man who never believed in God. He felt God never existed. He did all things with his own strength and he had succeeded all this while. One day, he had a problem at work and he was laid off. His wife was also a stay at home mom so things were truly difficult. Suddenly, his strength could not carry him through. He was totally worn out. He was so confused. His kids were at home because he couldn't pay their fees that term, feeding had even become a luxury. His hope was revived when a friend promised to lend him some money. All of a sudden, his friend was not picking his calls. He tried to communicate with his friend but all efforts proved futile. What do I do now? He said to himself quietly. Reality had begun to stare in his face. For the first time in his life, he broke down and said a simple prayer to God. What had he done? He had just prayed and he was surprised at himself. An hour later, he begun scrolling through the contacts on his phone and a name highlighted. He hadn't spoken to this person in two years. Something was urging him to call that number. He finally did and the person invited him into his office. When he got there the man was asking of his kids, he told the man, how the kids were at home because of his inability to pay fees. The man didn't utter a word, pulled out money in a brown envelope from his drawer and handed over to him. He took it and left for home. When he got home, he called the man and thanked him so much for the kind gesture. Guess what? The money was enough to pay the kids fees for a whole year. He told him, if he had tried to thank him, he would have broken down. Anthony now believes in God and most importantly the power of Prayer and that God loves a contrite heart.

"The Sacrifices of God are a broken spirit, A broken and a contrite heart-These, O God, You will not despise" Psalm 51:17

ABIDING HEART-BE GOD'S FRIEND

By abiding in His word when we pray, we constantly and continually depend on him no matter the situation and we learn to be content whatever the circumstances. In John 15 Jesus said "I am the true vine he who abides in me will bear fruit, one part that excites me anytime I am reading John 15 is in verse 7 is that ***if you abide in me, and my words abide in you, you will ask what you desire, and it shall be done for you. David in the bible was a man with an abiding heart***. David was a man after God's own heart. David loved God and God loved him because he consulted God every day for his destiny to be fulfilled. Are we talking to God every day? When we talk to God every day, He is with us through our journey and He guides us every step of the way. Even when David took another man's wife (Bathsheba) to be his wife and had her husband (Uriah) killed. God's wrath came upon David and he was punished. He fled from his son Absalom and his throne. Through the punishment, David had an abiding heart and God was his "All in All". He still prayed to God continually mostly through his songs. He waited patiently for the Lord to restore his throne and the Lord did at His time. Who would have thought that David, God's friend will go through rejection, persecution, harassment and so much suffering? The fact that God loves us doesn't mean we wouldn't face trials of any kind. Even in trials we should remain in the Lord. As Christians we don't only share in God's glory but also suffer for Christ's sake. Michael was a man who always used his strength in all things. He was a contractor who always used his connections to get contracts. He knew almost everybody. There was one contract that he wanted, that he could not get. He tried to get that contract through the people he knew but this time it didn't work. He became very frustrated. This contract will be an end to his problem. I told Michael about God and told him, why you don't ask this helper I know and trust that he will do it. Okay he said, reluctantly. He still tried using people to help him get in, the frustration was getting worse. So he prayed and asked God to help him get that contract. After some days, Michael met me and said; Adwoba, I have prayed but God hasn't answered. Then I said, wait. You need to abide in God. What is abiding he said, then I answered praying and dwelling in the word of God constantly, continually and depending on only Him to do it. Wow! He exclaimed, this is going to be difficult. Then I said, it is the grace that will carry you through not your works. He confessed to me that it was difficult at first, but later on it became part of him. The grace of the Lord was flowing from his being not his doing. He went about his normal jobs. He was there one day, when he received a call from the very company he wanted to go to. He couldn't believe It, God had done it. How his phone number went there, he had no idea. God really surprised him. From that day until now, He really believes in abiding in the Lord. Now everything you say, he says "go and abide in the Lord "earning the name "Uncle Abide."

There is total completeness in the Lord. John 15 was an instruction that Jesus gave on how we should live our lives in order to be fruitful. ***Proverbs 28:9 says if anyone turns a deaf ear to my***

instruction, even their prayers are detestable. Abiding in Him is remaining in Jesus Christ for His glory to be manifested in His time. When you abide in Jesus Christ, He comforts you in every situation. Are you lost in the world? Is your world crumbling? Life is full of complexities that sometimes we find ourselves embittered in a problem in one way or another. Do you feel like nothing makes sense anymore? You have tried all solutions, it is just not working. You feel like giving up on life. Friends and family have dejected you. You suddenly feel you are at emptiness' stage. Checking again, you just turned thirty and have a couple of grey hairs in your head and you are worried. In Matthew 6:27, ***Jesus said; can anyone of you by worrying add a single hour to your life?*** Try prayer through Christ Jesus for in Him there is hope. He will help you be the change that you need, for Christ in you, the hope of glory. James said in Chapter 1:2-*3 **"My brethren count it all joy when you fall into various trials knowing that the testing of your faith produces patience. But let patience have its perfect work, that you may be perfect and complete lacking nothing".***

Jesus Christ is your comfort in all things. He is the one who can comfort you so that you can lend a comforting hand to others when the need arises. 2 Corinthians 1;3 says ***"Blessed be the God and Father of our Lord Jesus Christ, the father of mercies and God of all comfort who comforts us in our tribulation that we may be able to comfort those who are in any trouble with the comfort with which we ourselves are comforted by God.***

John was wrongly accused of embezzling some funds in the Insurance Company where he worked. He has worked there all his adult years and rose to the position of an Assistant Manager. His wife, Victoria was a stay at home mom with five kids when John was laid off. For John being employed again was unsuccessful owing to the bad record he had. Surprisingly, Victoria couldn't find a job too. They sold almost all their properties to make ends meet. For three years, they depended on friends and family for their upkeep. Their friends and family were also getting tired of supporting them. The lovely home Victoria and her husband shared has turned into something else with constant fighting and nagging. I met Victoria through a friend and immediately our friendship begun. I told her about making God her "All dependency". I said to her one afternoon that the secret to receiving miracles from God is to abide in Him. Gradually Victoria shifted her focus from friends and family that could help her out of her situation and focused on God entirely. It wasn't easy, I told her abiding in God is frustrating but God is there with you. Out of the blue there would be donations and gifts to her that she knew nothing about. After a while, she called me one evening to tell me how her husband has been reinstated back into the job and has even been compensated for being wrongfully accused. I cried that day, I was so happy. Victoria's secret to her miracle was to abide in the Lord.

John 10:31-32: To the Jews who had believed him, ***Jesus said, if you hold to my teaching, you are really my disciples. Then you will know the truth, and then the truth will set you free.***

FAITHFUL HEART
A SIP BECOMES A GULP

Psalm 37:5 "Commit your way to the Lord, trust Him and He will do this."

I once worked as an intern in one of the social security firms in the country. A law student who was visually impaired was seeking for student loan to pay off her tuition. She was such a lovely young girl who always beamed with smiles anytime she came to the office. I happened to be the customer care representative working on her documents; we therefore developed a beautiful relationship. Anytime we finished working on her documents, I took her to the roadside and put her in a taxi and she went home. This I did for a long time. She therefore developed that trust in me and anytime she passed by the office, I escorted her to the roadside/ bus stop. Even when I wasn't in the office owing to official errands, she waited for me to return and I escorted her to the roadside as usual. I had become her only trusted escort. Although, she had never seen me, she believed I will take her safely to her destination. She was exercising faith in me. It started as a one-time thing and it gradually developed into this big trust. That is the faith that God wants us to have. He knows it is difficult to trust Him fully, but little by little as we put our trust in him we overcome our fears, so that we can fully have faith in Him. God wants us to trust Him and have Faith in all things for we are safe in his arms.

Trusting the only true God that whatever decision he makes is final and it is best for you is faith. Sometimes when we pray, we want results, and we at times limit God with our prayers. Most times, what we are praying for becomes a 'do or die' situation. Sometimes the cooked rice is spoilt, so you just have to have faith and wait for a new one which is being cooked and it will be served at the right time.

Faith was a very brilliant girl who had a Master's degree in Economics. Faith felt that what would make her life complete was a job. She applied to one of the Universities to be an Assistant Registrar. She was called for relieving duties from that same University and she felt that was a quick and sure way of getting for the job. After three months, the contract ended and she went home so sad. Why was she not taken? I have worked so hard, she said quietly to herself. A few months later, Faith was called for an interview for the Assistant Registrar job. She was so happy and her joy knew no bounds. She quickly prepared for the interview and went for the interview so confident. The questions started and she realized she could not answer them. She had suddenly forgotten all what she learnt. She left for home suddenly and she was never called for the appointment for months. She called back and the feedback she received was that, she didn't get the job. Which was quite expected because she knew her performance at the interview wasn't that good. She went home so sad and her wish was that the University will call her back for the job; suddenly a still small voice started echoing "live your name". She got the message so clearly that "have faith" how can I have faith in such a situation, she said. She decided to have faith but somehow along the line her faith was challenged and she grew distant from God. Somehow, she had a glimpse of hope in the Lord. After 6 months she had a call from a Company she had never applied to giving her a job offer with juicy fringe benefits. She couldn't believe it. Although her faith was challenged and she got disturbed, she still had hope in God and God was God in this situation.

The Helpline is Engaged

"We are hard-pressed on every side, yet not crushed; we are perplexed, but not in despair". 2 Corinthians 4:8.

Just have faith that God is omniscious (He is all Knowing) *James 5; 15 says the prayer offered in faith will make the sick person well; the lord will raise them up, if they have sinned, they will be forgiven.*

In the early hours of Good Friday in 2011, I woke up with the most confused look ever. I was in labour with my second child and I didn't see it coming. The mucous plug had come out but there were no contractions. So I rushed to the hospital, when I got there, the hospital was very quiet and I wondered. Then I realized that the workers were on break for the Easter. I even forgot it was Easter! How could I? I have been nesting LOL. The Doctor on duty examined me and said oh I cannot feel your baby. Then I gasped! Really! I don't believe it! Do you feel the baby he asked? Yes, I replied faintly. I was losing hope then I pulled myself together and said to myself, my baby cannot die like that, it just cannot happen. I quietly said a heartfelt prayer to God and immediately my faith grew and my strength was renewed. Then the Doctor came with all his gadgets and performed an examination on me and said Oh! The baby is alive! I quickly smiled and said I was never going to fall for that. I really had FAITH! Some hours later, there were still no contractions, I was just worn out. So they had to induce labour and the pain was very excruciating. After going through all that and with God by my side I pushed out the most beautiful baby girl I had ever seen, a precious gift from God. God blessed me with the perfect gift ever, I was so overwhelmed. My sufferings turned out to be a blessing and most importantly my faith in God heightened and I believed Him without any reasonable doubt. Hebrews 11:6 sums it all up by saying *"And without Faith, it is impossible to please God, because anyone who comes to Him must believe that He exists and that He rewards those who earnestly seek Him".*

THANKFUL HEART-THE GLASS IS HALF FULL

When we are faced with certain challenges in life, we forget what God has done for us and we tend to focus on the problem which makes us so ungrateful. Let's start looking at the glass half full instead of half empty. We should learn how to praise God and give all strength to him.1 Thessalonians 5:18" *Give thanks in all circumstances, for this is God's will in Christ Jesus".* A good friend of mine was in dire need of money to feed his children. He had to visit his children that day and give them some financial support. He didn't have anything on him. He was downhearted, how will my children eat? He thought to himself. He knelt down and begun singing a song of praise. The song was about Jesus being the good shepherd. Then the Holy Spirit whispered to him. Do you think the good shepherd will not look after his sheep? Within minutes he heard the message tone on his phone. It was a text message of an old friend who had sent him money. He couldn't believe his eyes. In times of hardship, when we sing praises instead of complaining, God comes through for us. Jesus is really the good shepherd. Let us cling to him and He will take care of his sheep.

I am the good shepherd; and I know my sheep and am known by my own. (John 10:14).

EVERY DAY IS A MIRACLE.

We are always waiting for the "big things" to happen to us so that we can bare our testimonies that God truly lives, what of the "little things " that keeps us going each day. A lady had a very loving husband who was the toast of all single women in the neighbourhood where they lived. This lady had no child and she wanted one so badly. She not able to have a child, was affecting her so badly that it was tearing her marriage apart. Her only focus was how to get this "miracle" baby. She felt she has been neglected by God and grew so distant from her family and of course she neglected her duties at home. She was breaking the heart of her family and most importantly her husband. Thereafter, her husband was diagnosed of Cancer. She began to see things differently." Life "had become important to her than anything else. She prayed fervently for God to heal her dying husband. Unfortunately, her husband lost the battle with cancer and died. After her husband's death, she realized how she had not been thankful enough to God for all the wonderful things around her and most importantly for "life".

You either live by the fact that every day is a miracle or every day is no miracle. Let's learn to appreciate the little things we have, for God is everywhere working miracles for us. Let us thank God when we get up in the morning, when we drop our kids off at school, when we arrive safely at work, when we get back home safely. Let us look at our families, coworkers, friends and neighbours and thank God for this wonderful people He has given us to affect each other's lives. Life is indeed a blessing.

"Bless the Lord, O my soul and forget not all His benefits" Psalm 103:2

PURE HEART

Blessed are the pure in heart, for they shall see God. (Matthew 5:8)

Luke 18:19 says, No one is good except God alone. Let's come to God in sincerity in prayer irrespective of how unrighteous we feel we are. *Hebrews 10: 22 tells us to draw near to God with a sincere heart in full assurance of faith, having our hearts sprinkled to cleanse us from guilty conscience and having our bodies washed with pure water.* Peter was a man with so much faith and hope in God. Everything was going on so smoothly in his life. Until his world started crumbling. He begun to lose everything he had. He suddenly became unemployed; he got separated from his wife and was now living with an extended family member. He had borrowed money to keep up with his living expenses; everybody felt he was a nuisance. Times were hard; it really was, he felt so dejected. His friends and family had all left him.

When he was alone, he sat down quietly and wondered WHY GOD HAS LEFT HIM? He felt God was missing in his life. The more he thought about his situation, the angrier he got. He couldn't pray, reading the bible has suddenly become a chore he no longer wanted to engage in. the straw that broke the camel's back, was when his phone also got spoilt. The only means of hope was gone. How can he receive feedback from the many employers he had applied to for a job? He was totally worn out.

One day, he carried his sim card in his pocket and strolled over to an Auntie who runs a shop by the roadside. He entered the shop and said Auntie, I just popped in to say hello. The Auntie replied, I have been looking for you, I have called your phone severally but it wasn't going through. Then Peter told him, about his ordeal. Then the Auntie gave him a phone to use for the mean time. Immediately, he activated his number, a call came through. The man at the other end of the phone said. Are you Peter? Then he replied, yes. Then the man continued, we are calling from this company and I am offering you a job. Can you come for your appointment letter? He hanged up shockingly, borrowed money from his auntie and left. His job offer was the most lucrative ever and he even felt he didn't deserve it. His first salary was able to pay back all the money he owed and even had more to spare.

He called me and said, Adwoba, I can't explain it! This is God! I said; you gave up on him but he never gave up on you. All along He was working something bigger for you.

"And we know that all things work together for good to those who love God, to those "who are the called according to His purpose" **(Romans 8:28)**

A TRUE PRAYER
COME AS YOU ARE
The Samaritan Woman at the Well

In John Chapter four, there was an account of Jesus and the Samaritan woman at the well. Jesus asked for a drink of water from the Samaritan woman. The woman was surprised that a Jew could ask a Samaritan for a drink, for Jews did not associate with Samaritans at that time. A conversation then followed between Jesus and the Samaritan woman. Jesus answered her in verse ten that ***if you knew the gift of God and who it is that asks you for a drink, you would have asked him and He would have given you living water.*** Jesus told her later on that everyone who drinks water from the well will be thirsty again but whoever drinks the water He gives them will never thirst. He concluded by saying that the water will become in them a spring of water welling up to eternal life. The woman then asked Jesus for His water. The woman was truthful to Jesus when he asked about her husband. It was shameful to be married five times at that time and still be unmarried. However, the woman was very truthful despite her shame. She came to Jesus in truth; just as she was. In verse 23 to 24 Jesus said ***"yet a time is coming and has now come when the true*** *worshipers will worship the Father in the Spirit and in truth, for they are the kind of worshipers the Father seeks. God is spirit and His worshipers must worship in the Spirit and in truth".*

When praying to our Father in heaven, irrespective of our shame, we must come to God in prayer, just as we are with a sincere heart. There should be no cover ups just like the Samaritan woman who bared it all at Jesus' feet in order to get living water. For this is the kind of worshipers that God wants.

After presenting your request before God from your heart, pray in the spirit and through Christ according to the perfect will of God. *In John 14:6, Jesus said I am the way, the truth and the life no one cometh to the father but by me.* Before you pray through Christ you have to accept him as your personal savior in your hearts and soar on the wings of the Holy Spirit. Even in our imperfections, the benefits of a personal relationship with God surpass all things. *Prayer ultimately builds upon the foundation that Christ laid for a fulfilled life.*

CHAPTER SIX
GOD'S ANSWER

When you have a case and you send it to court, do you settle the case yourself? Or you trust the court's decision. That is the same way with God. When we pray, we have to wait for God's answer. We do not have to try and solve the case ourselves. We take God's decision in good faith, trusting that it is the best for us even though we may not see it as such.

Matthew 7:7 says "Ask and it shall be given to you, seek and you will find, knock and the door will be opened to you." God always answers prayers. The answer lies solely with God. Whatever answer He has for you, He prepares you for the answer. David was prepared for the throne in the wilderness; to humans nothing was being done. Sometimes He says wait, I have a better plan. At other times He says no, it would not help you, at other times He says yes. Unfortunately, it is the yes, we always want to hear and at our scheduled time.

FIXING THE BROKEN LEG OF THE TABLE

The table is the foundation where food is put, if one of the legs is broken when you put food on it, it will pour. And when it does you cannot pick it up, it will be all dirty and cannot be eaten. When you try eating it the germs will destroy you. So the legs of the table should be fixed and stable so that the food will not pour.

God can always do anything at the snap of His fingers but somehow we are not ready. People may ask why I am not ready. The broken leg of the table has to be fixed. In sum, the Christ factor is not there.

Myron was a brilliant chap who was addicted to drugs. The drugs had begun to destroy his organs. In short Myron was dying. Myron loved God. To help the underprivileged was his passion. Unfortunately, any money he had he took to drugs. Myron loved life; he wanted a family so badly. He prayed to God for a wife. The answer was NO. Why did God say no, Myron loved God but a wife will be so bitter getting married to a drug addict? Myron needed to fix his life before a wife is given. He needed Christ to take away the addiction. Myron finally found Christ, a few years down the line he got married to a beautiful lady and his addiction to drugs was no more. When Myron made Christ the center of his life, Jesus fixed the leg of the broken table and now his marriage had the proper foundation to thrive on and his life was restored.

RESTING IN THE FINISHED WORK OF GOD

We at times miss God's answer when we pray forgetting the fact that it is only the grace that will make it happen and He works in you not the other way round. A young man prayed and prayed for a job. He never believed that God will do it. So he went about soliciting for help although he had prayed. One day, he went out as usual soliciting for help and the home phone rung. It was a company wanting to employ his services. He wasn't there. They gave a message to the wife, to tell him about them wanting to employ his services. His wife called and called only to hear his phone ringing underneath the rug in the hall. He was so much in a hurry that, he had left his phone. Now how to reach him had become a dilemma, for there was a deadline for him to report to the headquarters of the company. The deadline was 2 pm in the afternoon. Unfortunately, all efforts to reach him proved futile. In the evening, he came home so tired and told his wife how he had misplaced his phone. His wife sighed and said you missed a very important call, your phone was underneath this rug, then his wife, took the phone and gave it to him and told him about the call. The young man didn't know what to do. He had missed God's call by not relying on the grace but on his works.

Romans 11:6 say" And if by grace, then it is no longer of works; otherwise grace is no longer grace. But if it is works, it is no longer grace; otherwise work is no longer work".

JESUS, IS THE GOOD SHEPHERD

I am the good shepherd; the good shepherd lays down his life for the sheep. (John 10:11)

Furthermore, God sometimes uses people to answer our prayers. There was a time when I was used to answer someone's prayer. Mary had come to City, to seek greener pastures. She had a toddler of about 18 months which her boyfriend had abandoned. She came to live with a distant uncle. One afternoon, I called a friend of mine and said, I wanted a hairdresser to braid my kid's hair for school, and then she said, I have the perfect hair dresser for you. Mary was brought to me and she braided my kid's hair so beautifully. Wow! I said to myself, what a talented girl? I paid her for her services. I realized that her toddler's dress was all torn and tattered. So I quickly rushed into my bedroom and gave her two packs of diapers and some clothes for the baby. As I picked the baby I realized, she was so light so I gave her food and the way the baby gulped down the milo, I was so amazed. Then I felt, I should give this girl more food, so I went into my kitchen and gave her some groceries so she could make some food for herself and her baby when she gets home. Mary broke down and cried, and then she told me how she had prayed all night yesterday because she didn't know where her next meal was coming from. She went on and said the diaper on the baby was the last one she had. Tears streamed my eyes, have I been used to answer someone's prayer? I just looked up and thank God. I was glad; I was able to help when I could. Jesus said, in Matthew 25:40 **_Truly, I tell you whatever you did for one of the least of this brothers and sisters of mine you did it for me"_**.

THE SERVANT IS THE GREATEST

On another note a lady told me a story of how she got her dream job through helping a complete stranger. She had prayed for a job change and there was no answer. This is her narration:

As I walked home from church last night, I found someone sobbing in the dark. Who could be sobbing at this time of the night? I was afraid but I wanted to find out why she was crying. So I drew near her with caution. I got close and I realized that it was a woman in her late 30's. Why are you crying I asked? She did not answer. I repeated the question again and she told me how her husband had thrown her out that night. Since she was a stay at home mom she doesn't know what to do or where to go. I asked about her children. Then she told me her kids were with a friend nearby. I stayed in a huge apartment and had one room vacant. So I told her I will give her and her two kids a place to stay. She couldn't believe what she was hearing. I held her hand, comforted her and we went for her two kids. We took her luggage and left to my house. That was the story of how I completely took a whole stranger in. To cut a long story short, this stranger connected me to my dream job that I have always thought about. Sometimes, it pays to get out of your comfort zone and help someone. It will create an inconvenience for you but it will go a long way to help you, best of all it could be your answer to your prayer. God works in diverse ways and we are not supposed to know which way our prayers will be answered. Just allow yourself to walk through the journey. For the journey with Christ is more important than your goal, owing to the fact that He sees the perfect picture.

Jesus washing the feet of the disciples was a pure act of humility, which as servants of God; we should all emulate this great act. Jesus is Lord and Master, He never lewd His authority over His disciples but rather demonstrated a great act of lowliness.

A lady lived near a man who was sick and had been shunned by his family and friends. She willingly took care of this man who had a nauseating and stinky smell. Eventually the man was healed of whatever sickness it was. The man in return gave her a house in an urban area that she never asked off and was not even expecting. This lady was humble enough to engage in this act of compassion. Her deeds paid off in a surprising way. Her house was in foreclosure and that was exactly what she needed. An act of humility and kindness was the way to go for her.

Proverbs 29:23 a man's pride shall bring him low: but honor shall uphold the humble in spirit.

DON'T TRY TO UNDERSTAND GOD

The following story tells how God is sovereign and so vast. We should not interfere with His sovereignty.

I was in the kitchen, cooking my favourite meal when the home phone rung. I grabbed the napkin close by the sink and cleaned my hand. I then picked up the phone. Hello, I answered, the voice on the other end said; is this Mrs. Johnson? I replied in the affirmative. Ok Mrs. Johnson, she continued, we are calling you in connection with a job you applied two years ago. Are you still interested? I said yes. Could you please come for an interview tomorrow? I said ok. What time? 8. 00 a.m. she concluded. When I hanged up, my heart sank. I haven't worked in two years. I prayed so much for this job, which I even gave up. Why didn't they call me earlier, this is a wrong time to call me for a job. I am five months pregnant! I stopped cooking, picked some books and started preparing for the interview anyway. Afterwards, I went into my closet and found a dress that could hide my bump; I matched it with a pretty coat. I was really showing and I realized no dress was hiding my bump. Ok, I said, when I go to the interview, if she realizes I am pregnant that's ok. Who could hide a five months pregnancy anyway? I went to the office premises very early and waited for the interview to start. I was eventually called and my interview begun. During the interview, the interviewer started looking at my bump, I felt so uncomfortable. When my interview ended, I knew I wasn't getting the job, obviously, she has found out that I was pregnant. Two weeks after, I had a call whilst shopping at my favourite grocery shop that I had the job. I was confused: why did I get the job? Didn't they see that I was pregnant? I started having mixed feelings. It didn't feel so good. So I set out the next day to work, my first day. I got there very early again and waited for an orientation. A lady walked to me and said we are sorry, there is a training programme and we will like you to take part. That was how I was thrown into the job. Officially, I had started work. I worked for about two weeks, when the director asked me if I was pregnant. She said she never knew I was pregnant. I was so shocked. The God that we serve is so great. If he wants to do something for you, He will do it no matter the circumstances. Sometimes our inner self is our stumbling block or our greatest obstacle. Based on our experiences and the conditions that we are in, we feel the answer to our prayer should go this way or that way. God is sovereign! ***1 Corinthians 2:11 says " for who knows a person's thought except their own spirit within them, in the same way no one knows the thoughts of God except the spirit of God."***

AN INSTANT GOD

Sometimes God answers instantaneously. When I was pregnant with my third child, I was past my due date I was feeling so uncomfortable. I wanted my baby to be out. The Doctor had said we will try other alternatives of the baby coming out if the baby doesn't come out naturally I didn't want to go under the knife. So I closed my eyes and prayed. Within five minutes I was in labour. I gave birth a few hours later. This was one of the easiest births I had ever had.

HE COMES THROUGH AT THE RIGHT TIME

There is no "when" in God's Calendar. God is timeless; in your wait, there is an assurance that no temptation will come that is beyond what you can survive if you are God's child. He knows how far you can travel. In your human limitations there are times you feel you are overstretched. He only allows us to handle only the one's we can to a point. God is faithful, it won't break you down. He always comes through for us! The story of Lazarus, in John chapter 11, tells us about how Lazarus was sick and Mary and

Martha sent for Jesus to come. To Mary and Martha, Jesus came a bit too late because Lazarus had been dead for four days, but to Jesus it was the ***perfect timing for the son of God to be glorified through it.*** In chapter 21, "Now Mary said to Jesus, Lord, if you had been here, my brother wouldn't have died, but even now I know that whatever you ask of God, God will give you. Jesus said, I am the resurrection and the life, "he who believes in me, though he may die, he shall live". Jesus raised Lazarus from the dead at the right time. The time you want your prayer to be answered may not be His time. We often get bored whilst waiting for God to do something for us. You are not alone. Don't give up. It is definitely not just waiting that matters but it is how you behave whilst waiting. In waiting, just remain in the lord by constantly praying, dwelling in the word of God and solely depending on Him. Yes, it is hard but it is worth the wait. You will be happy you did. Can you imagine what you would have lost if you didn't wait. At times we wonder why we have to wait so long only to discover that He is cooking something BIG.

LOSING TO GAIN

A young lady in her thirty's wanted to marry at all cost. Her boyfriend wasn't popping the question. She had prayed about it and was getting frustrated. She felt her biological clock was ticking. She needed to settle down and make babies. Eventually the question was never popped and the relationship was finally over. She channeled all her energy into schooling and came out with a PhD degree. She found a decent job in the community where she lived. As luck will have it all, she met a man she deeply fell in love with. Within a year of dating, they had gotten married. She knew this was the right fit for her and her past lover would have surely been a mistake. After a while she heard that her ex-boyfriend had passed owing to drug overdose. She was stunned and grateful to God for a wonderful escape. So we see how God sometimes tells us to wait and that He has a better option.

In another story, A man's kids were sacked from school for non- payment of fees. He didn't know where to turn to. He prayed to God to settle the school fees for the kids. The money for the fees was not coming. He felt God has unanswered his prayer. His kids could not go to school for three weeks. He unexpectedly had money to pay the fees. The duration of not getting the money was so long that he had already started homeschooling the kids. That was the birth of a great school. When he wanted money to pay fees, the money delayed and his talent that was hiding was unearthed. God gave him a better option. ***Many are the plans in a man's heart, but it is the Lord's purpose that will prevail.*** (Proverbs 19: 21)

MISFORTUNES CAN BE ANSWERS

A misfortune can be blessings in disguise. I had made earlier arrangements for a taxi driver to pick me to work since there was no bus service where I lived. On that fateful day, I called the taxi driver telling him to pick me up. He answered by saying that he couldn't make it. What a disappointment? I didn't know what to do; the time was too short for me to make another arrangement so I decided to walk out of the house hoping I may find an empty taxi. As I was about to cross the road, I saw a taxi far off. So I waited for it to draw near. As it drew near, I realized that the taxi was empty, and then I stopped the car. I politely asked the driver whether it could take me to where I was going, he replied in the affirmative. As I sat down in the car, I asked the driver whether he normally came this way. He said; no madam, I just took this turn not knowing why. I said quietly to myself, God thank you. So we engaged in a conversation and he told me about a two bedroom house he was looking for someone to rent. I have been looking for an apartment, I told him. Guess what, the house was so close to my place of work and the price was very low compared to other two bedroom house. To crown it all, my taxi fares were also off. Sometimes, things that we think are disappointments are actually blessings in disguise. He knows what He is doing and knows the future that we do not know. Let us learn to trust in Him fully.

PERMISSIVE WILL OF GOD

Keep on knocking and let the door be opened to you. Don't try and open the door yourself. How would you feel if you were knocking on someone's door and you forced yourself in without the person's permission? Disaster for short! You see an unwelcoming face starring at you in the door way. Before we even pray, we already have what we think should be the answer on our minds and the specific time for it and if it doesn't happen around that time we get so frustrated. Sometimes we want a particular answer at all cost and God grants us his permissive will and with that granted we bear the consequences ourselves.

Now in Genesis 15:4, God promised Abram that he will give him a son and he will be his heir. In Genesis 16 we were told that Abram could not wait and Sarai asked Abram to sleep with Hagar and she got pregnant. Hagar's son, Ishmael was God's permissive will. God allowed it even though it wasn't His will and even sent an angel to be with Hagar during her pregnancy and Ishmael had to live in hostility towards all his brothers.

I will relate God's permissive will to an event on one bright Valentine's Day morning. A young boy decided to wear a red long sleeves track suit to school in a very hot weather. His mother cautioned, son, are you going to wear this red long sleeves track suit in this weather, I have already picked a red t-shirt with short sleeves for you. I think it will be favourable for that weather. The son cried and cried and his mother had no choice but to grant his wish. He went to school happily but felt so uncomfortable and came back with heat rashes. He had to bear the consequences of his own action that is wearing that red track suit to school against his mother's wish. This is what we do after we pray we rush things so much that at the end of the day God grants us His permissive will and we bear the consequences. God is all knowing allow Him to bring a relief totally in His own time.

GOD'S PERFECT WILL

Philippians 1:4 states that ***"He who started a good work will bring it to completion"*** Although God promised Abram he will give him an heir. Abram was in disbelief, despite the fact that Sarai was past the age of childbearing. In Genesis 18:14 Sarai said "After I am worn out and my lord is old" Sarai herself believed it was impossible, in human minds it was never possible for Sarai to carry a child but with God it was. In Genesis 21, the lord was gracious to Sarai as he had said, and the lord did for Sarai what he had promised. The very time God promised him. God gave her a son.

After my Master's degree, I prayed for a PhD degree so I could be a college teacher. I then applied to my alma mater for my PhD degree. I went through all the processes. At the last stage, my interview wasn't successful. I was so downhearted. I so much wanted this PhD degree.it was a big blow to me. I blamed myself; I was so hard on myself. I said to myself, if only I had answered the questions this way, I could have gotten in. Years passed, after I had found Christ, I was checking my email when an advert popped up. I instantly knew it was God that has placed the advert there. It was school advertising for people to get in to do their PhD. I decided to apply. So I put in my application within three days I had gotten admission to do my PhD in a very prestigious university and guess what it came with full scholarship. To crown it all, the course was something I had passion for. Two weeks after, I had started classes. This testimony amazes me till date. We might have a plan but God's plan is what will prevail. Sometimes when we pray for something and we don't get it, God has something better for you. The timing is not right. When the timing is right, it looks like everyone is waiting for the king or queen.

WAITING FOR GOD'S TIMING

Jonas was a very industrious man; He worked very hard to cater for his family. Suddenly, things took a different turn and fending for his family had become so difficult. One day, Jonas called me and said; Adwoba, My landlady has increased the rent. Things are so difficult that I cannot even pay the old rent. I told Jonas to take his rent issue to God. He smiled and I immediately knew he wasn't going to do it. After two weeks, He came back again complaining, this time the landlady has decided to throw him out. He sobbed bitterly, where am I going with my family? I said it again; take your rent issue to God. This time, he felt a glimpse of hope and I knew he was going to do it. After a month, He came back again and said the landlady hasn't thrown me out yet but she is giving me pressure to pay the rent. I said again, let you go and let God take the pressure. He will help you through it. He took his mind off the rent amidst pressures from the landlady and surprisingly he wasn't thrown out. After six months of living in a house without paying rent, God showed up. He had a job and it came with accommodation.

For our light affliction, which is but for a moment, is working for us a far more exceeding and eternal weight of glory, while we do not look at the things which are seen, but at the things which are not seen. For the things which are seen are temporary, but the things which are not seen are eternal. (2 Corinthians 4:17-18).

CHAPTER SEVEN
THE VALUE OF PRAYER

Prayer is always needed, God values prayer so much, prayer always gets us closer to God, but it is His perfect will that stand. Let us learn to pray according to the will of God for at times we limit God with our prayers and he grants us His permissive will. God has perfect timing, wait. If your strength is gone ask Him for the renewal of strength. *You can do all things through Christ who strengthens you. (Philippians 4:13).* Our strength is in the word of God, In Romans 12; 2 it says "Do not conform to the pattern of this world but be transformed by the renewing of your mind. Then you will be able to test and approve what God's will is-his good, pleasing and perfect will. The power of prayer should never be underestimated. Prayer gets us close to our heavenly Father. When we start our day with prayer, one feels so relaxed that God is in control.

Whenever we are having challenges in life, when we pray, then we are trusting God irrespective of the situation at hand and our hope is renewed in the Lord.

God's sovereignty surpasses all things, let us acknowledge that fact and trust His answers for He sees the perfect picture that we do not see. Mark 10:27 says with man this is impossible, but not with God: all things are possible with God.

LET GOD IN

He makes all things beautiful in His own time. Learn to wait. Allow God's grace, mercy and His love to see our request through. God is a merciful God. God has mercy on those he wants to have mercy on and has compassion on those he wants to have compassion for. (Romans 9:15). When we are faced with a challenge in life that is when we feel the need to pray. God cares about our day to day activities, don't let Him out. Sometimes we take the problems we feel it's difficult to God and the ones that we feel it's not difficult, we try and handle it. God is a sovereign God and don't underestimate his sovereignty. Let Him handle the things we think is trivial as well as important. Note that God cares for all things so don't share the responsibility with God when making your requests. Don't go on like this: God, you take care of this because I cannot handle that but as for this one I can handle it is trivial, so allow me. Try and bring everything to God in Prayer. Hey! He cares so much about the little things such as "what am I wearing today?" yes He is so interested. Every little thing is his business. Quite relieved huh? 1 Peter 5: 7 says *"casting all your care upon Him because he cares for you"* Note the word" all" not "some" which means bring everything to Him in prayer.

Adding house chores to four children was an arduous task for me. I woke up one morning feeling so tired, but I still had work to do and it was so much! I didn't know where to start from but I started anyway, in the middle of the chores, I was so overwhelmed and I asked God in prayer to help me with my chores. Honestly, He did! All of a sudden I felt someone was holding my hand to do the chores. I felt His strength everywhere, obviously I was so weak. The chores were done in no time and I just couldn't believe it. Paul said *"But He said to me, "My grace is sufficient for you, for my power is made perfect in weakness. Therefore I will boast all the more gladly about my weaknesses, so that Christ's power may rest on me. (2 Corinthians 12:19).* He loves you so much so turn all your cares and worries into Prayers.

WHATEVER GOD DOES IS GOOD

A friend's wife was critically ill whilst pregnant. We prayed about it all the time. Somehow we were scared that she would not make it but we kept hope alive. For in Christ our hope is always renewed and we are also strengthened. A week before her due date, she was induced and she gave birth to a beautiful baby girl. A baby girl she has always dreamed of having. We were all so happy and she was overjoyed. We were all relieved and happy that she made it. In a sudden twist of events, she got critically ill again three days after giving birth .She was rushed to the hospital in an ambulance our hopes were dashed again. What went wrong we asked ourselves? Did we not pray enough? Is there something we should have done that we did not do? We were filled with questions, obviously without getting answers. Her health deteriorated and she was on life support for two days. She passed away sadly and left a week old baby behind. The post mortem report stated that she died of hepatitis B. The husband was so devastated; he thought God has not been fair to him. Sometimes, death is an answer to our prayer. The answer to our prayer lies solely with God *for just as the Father raises the dead and gives them life; even so the son gives life to whom He is pleased to give it. (John 5:21).*

The righteous perish, and no one takes it to heart; the devout are taken away, and no one understands that the righteous are taken away to be spared from evil. (Isaiah 57:1)

After praying go to rest whilst God goes to work and take rest in Jesus Christ and trusting him that He will do it according to His will not our will. We always want to work for God instead of allowing God to take control and solving it for us. Let the word of God dwell in you, *for the word of God is alive and active. Sharper than any double-edged sword, it penetrates even to dividing soul and spirit, joints and marrow; it judges the thoughts and attitudes of the heart.* (Hebrews 4:12). By so doing, you can have some comfort, strength and the patience to wait for God's timing and his ultimate answer. You can only achieve this by turning your back against the world and concentrating on God only by abiding in Him. Our ever helper the Holy Spirit will guide you to understand the word, praying continually and living a Christ filled life. So that the only voice that guides you is the voice of God so His glory can be experienced. God's plan is so perfect. Could you imagine what you would have missed if you had God's permissive will. You can live out in frustration all your life. Humble yourself under God's mighty hand so that he can lift you up in due time." *And we know that in all things God works for the good of those who love him. Who have been called to according to his purpose*" (Romans 8: 28).

HIS WAY IS NOT YOUR WAY

God placed Moses in Egypt to deliver the Israelites from Pharoah. In Exodus 2: 11-22, Moses saw two people fighting and he took the law into his own hands and killed the Egyptian. When Pharoah was looking for him to kill him because of the crime he has committed. He fled from Egypt to Midian. He immediately lost track of where his destiny lies when he was ruled by anger. He did not submit his ways before the Lord and he did things his own way. God being God, He still used him after he had prepared him in Midian by taking care of sheep. He grew out of his anger and depended on God solely. He learnt how to be compassionate, meek and not to rely on his own strength but God's, so that he could lead the Israelites out of Egypt. God always straightens our way in preparation for the answer.

I was called for an interview for a job, I had applied to. The interview was in two stages. The first one was a written interview. I went in and did the interview. The time was up and I submitted the exams paper. I headed home with full of hope of getting the job. When I opened the front door to my house, I realized that I had deviated from the answer. I sat in my couch very sad. How could I deviate? I said to myself: I am not getting the job; this was a highly competitive exam. I prayed about it too. Why did this happen? The next day I was called to write the exams again. I was so shocked. In spite of the fact that I already knew the question, I prepared ahead of time. When I got to the exams center, the secretary asked curiously: do you know the Director of the Company? I said no. then she said: this thing has never happened before. I don't know the kind of God you are serving. God never forgot me. If I had done the exams the first time the right way, I would not have passed. God gave me more time to prepare for the exams by allowing that deviation to come back fully prepared.

1 Corinthians 2: 16 "for who has known the mind of God so that we can instruct him? But we have the mind of Christ. Let us live in the known that Christ saves and not live in the fear of the unknown. The unknown is the future that belongs to God only.

BE IN GOD'S WILL

Let us not limit God with what we want. The helpline always goes through and it is always answered by God. If we open up to Him in spirit and in truth and we allow Him to work things out according to His will. How can we put ourselves in God's will? If your will is in God's will, it is like you are in a ship where Christ is the captain. He steers the ship in whatever direction He seems fit and you move along with Him. There may be storms, but with Christ in that ship, you will overcome that storm. When you feel like you do not want to be in His ship and you jump into the sea, then you are on your own. You don't allow Him to control your life anymore but He just watches you. Then again, when you realize that you are drowning and you reach out to Him for help. With your hand in His, He will pull out. But when you come back unto the ship, you will feel cold that is the consequences which you have brought upon yourself which you will bear alone but He will be with you and you will not be tempted beyond what you can bear. He always brings relief along the way; the relief is the towel to dry you up from the cold when you get on board. You will eventually get dry and you are in His ship again and He is at the wheel moving you again to the direction that is best for you.

DESIRING A RELATIONSHIP WITH THE FATHER

Anytime, my husband came home from work. He came with gifts for the kids and all the kids will shout his name happily in welcoming him. There was a time; he came home with no gifts. The kids were disappointed and the eldest child said; Daddy, you came home with nothing! The usual appellations from the other kids did not follow. The youngest child, who was a year old at that time, kept on shouting Daddy! Daddy! She wanted to be with her dad unconditionally. Are we calling on the name of God, just because we want gifts or because we want a relationship with him? Let us be like the one year old child and love God unconditionally, calling on His name because we want a relationship. In Mark 12: 41-44, we are told of the story of the widow who gave out all she had into the temple treasury. In monetary value, she gave just two coins but to Jesus, she gave the greatest. Out of her poverty, she sacrificed everything she had for the kingdom of God. Was she not thinking of saving the money for her basic needs? She put the kingdom first, by observing God's greatest commandment which is *Love the lord your God, with all your heart and with all your soul and with all your strength and with all your mind and love your neighbour as yourself.(Luke 10:27)* The money might be used for the poor like herself which is the love she has shown to people. *"Whoever claims to love God yet hates a brother or sister is a liar. For whoever does not love their brother and sister, whom they have seen, cannot love God, whom they have not seen".* (1 John 4:20) She also put her faith in Matthew 6:33-34 when dropping those last two coins. Which reads *"but seek first His kingdom and His righteousness, and all these things will be given to you as well. Therefore, do not worry about tomorrow, for tomorrow will worry about itself. Each day has enough trouble of its own.* Finally, *she set her mind on things above and not on earthly things.* (Colossians 3:2).Your prayer is a lifestyle with God; it is about how you live with Him all the time, having love in our hearts. May the peace of God be with us all as we continue to have a relationship with Him and be obedient to His will always, so that we may enter His rest. For anyone who enters God's rest also rests from their works, just as God did from His. (Hebrews 4:10). Therefore, since we have a great high priest who has ascended into heaven, Jesus the Son of God, let us hold firmly to the faith we profess. For we do not have a high priest who is unable to empathize with our weaknesses, but we have one who has been tempted in every way, just as we are—yet he did not sin. Let us then approach God's throne of grace with confidence, so that we may receive mercy and find grace to help us in our time of need. (Hebrews 4:14-16).

The Helpline is Engaged

www.ingramcontent.com/pod-product-compliance
Lightning Source LLC
Chambersburg PA
CBHW050618130526
44591CB00045B/2337